MW00324808

Redesign Your
Library Website

FOR REFERENCE

Do Not Take From This Room

OLATHE PUBLIC LIBRARY
201 EAST PARK
OLATHE, KS 66061

REDESIGN YOUR LIBRARY WEBSITE

Stacy Ann Wittmann
and Julianne T. Stam

LIBRARIES
UNLIMITED™

An Imprint of ABC-CLIO, LLC

Santa Barbara, California • Denver, Colorado

Copyright © 2016 by Stacy Ann Wittmann and Julianne T. Stam

All rights reserved. No part of this publication may be reproduced, stored in a retrieval system, or transmitted, in any form or by any means, electronic, mechanical, photocopying, recording, or otherwise, except for the inclusion of brief quotations in a review, without prior permission in writing from the publisher.

Library of Congress Cataloging-in-Publication Data

Names: Wittmann, Stacy Ann, author. | Stam, Julianne, author.
Title: Redesign your library website / Stacy Ann Wittmann and Julianne T. Stam.
Description: Santa Barbara, California : Libraries Unlimited, an imprint of ABC-CLIO,
    LLC, [2016] | Includes bibliographical references and index.
Identifiers: LCCN 2015043492 (print) | LCCN 2016005131 (ebook) |
    ISBN 9781440838569 (paperback : acid-free paper) | ISBN 9781440838576 (ebook)
Subjects: LCSH: Library Web sites—Design. | Library Web sites—United States—Case
    studies. | BISAC: LANGUAGE ARTS & DISCIPLINES / Library & Information Science /
    Administration & Management.
Classification: LCC Z674.75.W67 W58 2016 (print) | LCC Z674.75.W67 (ebook) |
    DDC 006.7—dc23
LC record available at http://lccn.loc.gov/2015043492

ISBN: 978–1–4408–3856–9
EISBN: 978–1–4408–3857–6

20 19 18 17 16   1 2 3 4 5

This book is also available on the World Wide Web as an eBook.
Visit www.abc-clio.com for details.

Libraries Unlimited
An Imprint of ABC-CLIO, LLC

ABC-CLIO, LLC
130 Cremona Drive, P.O. Box 1911
Santa Barbara, California 93116-1911

This book is printed on acid-free paper ∞

Manufactured in the United States of America

Stacy:

To Martha and Robert Wittmann, who reared me to believe that there is great empathy in the act of listening, and great wisdom to be found in the act of reading.

To Nora, I'm so glad you're my person.

To Julie, my partner in crime, marketing marvel, and dear friend, who encourages me to not be afraid to ask the tough questions and to expect an answer.

Julie:

To my husband Joe, who has been telling me for years that I should write a book, and who ended up having to put up with me doing only that for weeks on end. Thank you for always taking up the slack and for encouraging me in everything that I do.

To my parents, Bob and Mary, whose love and support have made every-thing I've achieved in life possible. Thank you for being wonderful role models.

To Jenny, my forever friend.

To Stacy, who is an inspiration to me as a librarian, as a manager, and as a mentor, and who is a great friend.

Contents

Preface

In October 2013, we gave a presentation at the Internet Librarian Conference in Monterey, California, on the redesign of our library website. Shortly after arriving back home, we received an e-mail from our editor, Barbara Ittner, suggesting that we write a proposal for a book based on our presentation and our website redesign experience.

We had decided to propose a presentation for the conference on the entire design process of a library website because that had been the presentation we were looking for when we attended the conference the previous year. When we were looking for information, we would have been very happy to have found a book that detailed the entire process of redesigning a library's website and all that it entailed. Barbara convinced us that others could benefit from our experience, and we submitted our proposal. It was accepted, and the result is this book that you hold in your hands.

We hope that you find this book to be a valuable resource as you embark on your website redesign. We would love to hear how you used what you learned here. Please feel free to contact us and let us know.

Stacy Wittmann
swittmann@gmail.com

Julie Stam
juliestam67@gmail.com

Acknowledgments

While the two of us were the webmasters for Eisenhower Public Library District's website during the 2012–2013 redesign process, there are many Eisenhower staff members who participated in the process of designing and creating our website. When we say "we" did something in this book, we are most often speaking of our website committee and/or the staff members who worked on and continue to work on the library's website, not just the two of us. We wish to acknowledge all of their hard work and dedication to the project.

Special thanks go to Dan McPhillips, the current head of the reference department, who became one of the webmasters when Stacy became the library director, and Christopher Clark, web and graphic designer for the library. We appreciate their continued efforts to ensure that our virtual presence is an accurate representation of our organization.

Thank you.

Stacy Wittmann and Julie Stam

1

Introduction

When we set out to manage the redesign of our library's website, we did what most information professionals do—we started doing research. We searched for articles, books, and people who could help us determine where to begin, what sort of timeline to establish, what sort of budget to establish, and how to determine content and design. While we found a couple of extremely valuable resources, there were not a lot of guides out there for people like us, librarians who were put in charge of redesigning a public library website who had very little experience with the process. This book is intended to serve as at least a starting point for the process, a map that lays out your options and points out the potential pitfalls and landmarks along the way.

One of the things we hear all the time from people who have no idea what it means to work in a library is, "you must get to read all the time." The likelihood is that if you are reading this book, you are a librarian and you know the sad truth. Librarians don't actually get a lot of time to read, at least not to read library-related materials.

One of our jobs in writing this introduction is to tell you why you should take precious time out of your day to actually read this book. Allow us to make the following case:

1. It's short. We know this is not a fascinating topic for most people, especially those people who are not web designers or architects by trade (which is why we assume you picked this book up in the first place). Therefore, we have done our best to make it as succinct and as helpful as possible. You are our people, we understand the limitations on your time, and we would rather you spend your non-work time relaxing with a beverage of your choice.

2. It not only lays out your options but also explains the time and budget commitments you will be making by deciding to redesign your website, as well as why you should do it. Again, we know your time is short and the

Figure 1.1 Eisenhower Public Library District Website

funds available to you for a project like this are even shorter. We don't want to waste your time or money.

3. You'll find out how to market the newly redesigned website. You'll learn how to identify your stakeholders. You'll also find out how you can prepare your public and your staff for the change, how to create user buy-in for both staff and patrons, and how to "manage up"—in other words, how to establish support from upper management.

Now, you may be wondering why you should pay any attention to us and what qualifications we have, if we are not web designers or engineers.

We are public librarians. That's pretty much it.

But we do have practical experience. Julie Stam is our marketing specialist. In addition to her master's in library and information science, she holds an MBA in marketing. In her former life, she was responsible for the social media and website upkeep at a local parochial school. She taught herself Joomla in order to create that website. Stacy Wittmann started out at Eisenhower Public Library District as the head of Reference Services and is now the director. As the head of reference services, she was responsible for the updating and maintenance of the library's website. Both have some (now mostly outdated) coding knowledge, enough to be a bit dangerous and to figure out how to "borrow" source code from here and there. Of course, our biggest bit of practical experience is facilitating the redesign of Eisenhower Public Library's website. Figure 1.1 shows what the website looks like today.

Essentially, this book is for anyone who is at a loss as to how to even begin figuring out how to do a redesign. No matter your budget, there is a solution that will enable you to produce a website that offers the most important things to your patrons:

> No matter your budget, there is a solution that will enable you to produce a website that offers the most important things to your patrons.

1. Information regarding location, hours, contact information, and programs;
2. Information regarding the administration of your library; and
3. Access to your online catalog, if you have one.

The trick is where to start and how to figure out which solution is best for you. If you don't have a lot of money, or no money at all, it's much simpler. It actually becomes more complicated if you have some money to throw at the problem.

We hope that, no matter what your budget is, you will find this information helpful at the very least as a jumping-off point. By the time you finish this book, we hope that you understand what your choices are, the potential time commitment involved for each choice, how to establish a reasonable budget and timeline, how to determine and produce your content, how to make sure your patrons know how to use the new site, and how to tell them about it.

Let's get started.

2

Why Does My Library Need a Website?

In 2016, it is surprising to encounter a business, organization, or governmental entity that does not have at least a basic web presence. Part of the benefit of using an app like Yelp, Foursquare, AroundMe, and other crowdsourced review services is that the user can navigate directly to a website to discover more information. A website factors into the customer's overall user experience. Under the best of circumstances, an entity's website can be used to execute a transaction from start to finish (i.e., purchasing a pair of shoes, ordering a meal for delivery, placing a book on hold). At minimum, if you have a brick-and-mortar location, you should have a website that conveys information like location, contact options, hours of operation, and a statement that identifies who you are and what you do.

It has become increasingly important for libraries to have a web presence. According to a study conducted by Pew Research Center, 87 percent of American adults now use the Internet (Fox & Rainie, 2014). Do you get 87 percent of your taxpayers to walk through the doors of your library? Probably not. That represents a significant number of the people who support you through tax dollars, and a website is a great way to at least get them to take a peek through a virtual door. Anecdotally, how often do you visit someplace new without checking to see if the place has a website? People are increasingly less inclined to spend time on an endeavor unless they are reasonably sure that the return on their time investment will be worth the effort.

When websites first became popular, libraries wanted a web presence in order to allow their patrons access to materials and information that could be made available virtually. Online patron access catalogs are perfect examples of this. What a delight to be able to search for something from home and know right away whether or not that item would be available when you walk through the door. As remote accessibility to online resources became more ubiquitous, the library website again was identified as the perfect vehicle to offer that service to the public. In addition, libraries, in their ongoing attempt to disseminate as much relevant information as possible, began providing links to community entities like utilities, village or city halls, churches, social services, and other entities that were deemed important to the quality of life of their public (Stover, 1997).

As librarians, we still want to offer access to patron access catalogs and databases. We also now have digital collections consisting of e-books, digital audiobooks, magazines, streaming video, and more that require an online platform. The question is no longer, do we need a website? Rather ask, how can we design a website that makes all these resources easy to find and use?

There is a constant struggle in web design for public libraries. You need to offer access to the catalog. You need to offer access to all of your digital resources. You are also required by law in many cases to provide information regarding

> The question is no longer, do we need a website? Rather ask, how can we design a website that makes all these resources easy to find and use?

budgets, boards of trustees and their activities, and other bits of information. Patrons want you to provide information on upcoming programs and available services. Finally, there is that content that you often want to provide that focuses on the expertise and enthusiasm of the librarians themselves. Features like staff blogs and suggested reading widgets are really fun and could potentially be useful for patrons. At what point, however, does the signal to noise become such that you end up burying our best content so deeply that no one who hasn't built the site can actually find it?

There is no magical formula to answer this question, and this is one reason why iterative design has become so important. Iterative design means that you make incremental changes that do not necessarily affect the overall functionality of the site, but that implement the results of constant usability testing in order to make the site more functional. Basically, the beauty of a website is that you can change it whenever you want. The trick is to make changes thoughtfully and deliberately. Ideally, however, you begin with a site that has good design and good content that will allow you to make those incremental changes along the way.

- DO decide that your library needs a website. Really. You really do have to have one now, and it needs to be good.
- DO carefully evaluate every element you decide to include on your website. How well does it serve the needs of your patrons? That book jacket carousel might look amazing, but can you maintain it so that it will be fresh every week or so? If not, skip it and feature staff picks that rotate once a month or so. It will make it more personal and you will be able to maintain it more easily. It could just be one or two titles that are

thoughtfully reviewed (not too wordy!), and it will still be more relevant than a river of months-old book jackets.

- DO conduct an even more careful evaluation of elements on your current website. Do you have analytics you can turn to in order to make a case for keeping something? Are the elements still relevant regardless of your analytics? I always say that it should hurt a little every time you withdraw an item from your collection. With websites, I believe the opposite is true. Less is more.

- DO think about surveying your public about your current website (if you have one) and what they would like to see on your website. Surveys require a good amount of planning, but can be a low-cost solution to acquiring valuable data from your users. Distribute it in-house (paper) and on your current website and Facebook page (you don't have a Facebook page? That's a whole different discussion).

- DO make sure that every element you include in your website accurately reflects who you are as an organization. You might have an old building, but your building isn't you, and you can still have an amazing website. Would people visiting your brick-and-mortar library wonder if they were in the wrong place if they only knew you previously through your website? Err on the side of them being wowed by your website, if you have to choose.

- DON'T dedicate primary real estate to extraneous material. Yes, have links to your park districts, utility companies, and so on, but do not place those links front and center. Save your primary real estate for the elements that people will come to your website to find—your calendar, your catalog, and your proprietary databases.

RESOURCES

Fox, Susannah and Lee Rainie. *The Web at 25 in the U.S.*, February 27, 2014, http://
www.pewinternet.org/2014/02/27/the-web-at-25-in-the-u-s.
Stover, Mark. *The Mission and Role of the Library Website*, 1997, http://misc
.library.ucsb.edu/universe/stover.html.

3

Our Website

Eisenhower Public Library District is situated in Harwood Heights, Illinois. We serve the communities of Norridge as well as Harwood Heights. Our two villages are completely surrounded by Chicago and located near O'Hare International Airport. Our library is funded by approximately 23,000 taxpayers, and a little more than half of them have library cards. Our budget is about $4,000,000 a year. Approximately 30 percent of our population is made up of native Polish speakers. About 25 percent of our population is 55 years or older. Most of them have a high school degree.

Eisenhower Public Library District started as a Project Plus "test" library in 1972. The residents of the two villages approved a referendum to support a district library through taxes in 1973. The library was originally situated in the basement of a local apartment complex and moved to a building that had been a sheet metal factory in 1974. The building was expanded and remodeled in 1982, going from 7,500 square feet to 11,250 square feet. In 1984, the library automated the collection, becoming the eighth library in the state to offer a computerized catalog. The library attempted and failed to pass a referendum for a new building twice, in 1997 and in 1998. A referendum for a new facility was finally passed in 2003. At long last, Eisenhower Public Library District opened the doors to its brand new, state-of-the-art, 44,500-square-foot facility on January 27, 2008.

There is no documentation marking the history of the library's website.

Figure 3.1 shows that the earliest capture of Eisenhower library's website by the Wayback Machine is from June 10, 2001.

Yeah, we know.

When Stacy started at the Eisenhower in 2006, the library had no databases linked on the website. The staff was unaware that remote access was included in their contracts for the most part. Also, can you see the link for

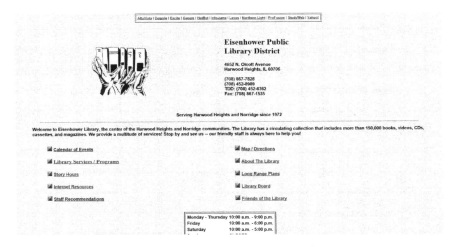

Figure 3.1 Early Version of Eisenhower Library Website

the catalog? No? That's because it's below the fold. That means that patrons had to scroll down to get to the one thing they likely wanted to use the most.

Figure 3.2 shows what the Wayback Machine captured a few years later. This is what our website looked like when we opened at our new location on January 27, 2008.

WE KNOW!

This version is marginally better. The link for the catalog is the first one you encounter at the top of the page, and again on the left. Overall, however, it is still dismally arranged and in no way reflected the quality of the library itself.

In early 2010, Stacy worked with a student in the Graduate School of Library and Information Science at the University of Illinois Urbana–Champaign (her alma mater) to do a partial redesign of the website as part of the student's curriculum. The redesign was the final project for the student; it did not cost the library any money. Figure 3.3 shows what the website looked like at the end of the project.

Figure 3.4 shows what the Chicago Public Library's (CPL) website looked like in 2010.

We've included the capture of the CPL website to illustrate the extreme difference between how a website can look when designed by a professional versus how it can look when designed by someone just learning and coding everything by hand. The Eisenhower library site did essentially what it was supposed to do, and it looked much better than it had previously, but at the time of launch it already looked out of date. The student had coded the entire thing, so we did not have a content management system to use, and no WYSIWYG (what you see is what you get) editor either. We had to have

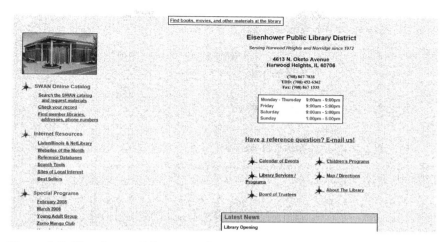

Figure 3.2 Eisenhower Library Website, January 2008

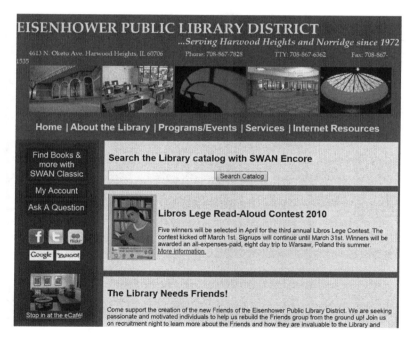

Figure 3.3 Eisenhower Library Website, 2010

Figure 3.4 Chicago Public Library Website, 2010

someone who knew HTML update the information on the home page, and any alteration to the basic design was nightmarish to consider.

In 2011, we conducted a user survey. One of the biggest responses we received from our patrons was regarding how outdated and clunky the website was, and how they expected a library such as ours to have a much "better" website. It was clear that the site was becoming something of a liability, so we finally made the decision to completely redesign the site. Julie came on board in 2012, occupying the fairly new position of marketing specialist, and the website became Julie and Stacy's first collaborative project.

As mentioned, we really didn't know where to start, so we began by discussing what we wanted, or thought we wanted, and what we didn't want. Our initial thought was that we would create a virtual branch. For those who are unaware of the concept of the virtual branch, it is essentially an extension of the business or organization that exists only in the virtual world (i.e., via the web or mobile devices at this point). It might not provide access to every service a brick-and-mortar location provides, but users can discover and access content immediately. Proprietary databases, downloadable digital books, digitized content, staff recommendations, and online library card registration would all be examples of services that make up a virtual branch.

We have heard some "bleeding edge" techies and designers disparage the concept as being outdated. Indeed, some of the ready-to-launch website options available present a more basic user experience, assuming that most people only visit a library website to find information about hours and location, and to search the catalog. This may be quite true in many cases. Anecdotally, as a reference librarian of over 15 years, Stacy has walked many patrons through the process of using online databases in the library so that they could use these resources from home. Likewise, if a database we subscribe to is experiencing downtime, we are more likely to find out about it because a patron called to let us know he or she cannot access it from home. Of course, we cannot possibly leave out the fact that many libraries now do have a digital collection of e-books and audiobooks, and unless a library's integrated library system or library management system allows authentication and downloading through the online catalog, the website is the primary access point to this collection for patrons.

Perhaps the most notable element that the concept of a virtual branch leaves out is the social one, which would enable users to comment, tag, subscribe, and contribute in general. In our experience, while you want to consider these options and capabilities, most library users tend to not look to library websites as a forum for connection with other users.

In conclusion, while this term is somewhat outdated, it still accurately describes how we envisioned people using the site: 24/7 access to digital content and information, with dynamic content that would draw the users in and compel them to dig around. We also wanted to expand our offering of virtual services, providing options like suggesting purchases, developing personalized reading lists, a read-alike generator, and options to sign up for in-person services through web forms.

In short, this is where we started from and where we thought we were going. Little did we know at the time that we were embarking on a journey of a project and would need to find our way through a number of challenges. We will unpack these challenges and what we discovered in the next several chapters.

- DO be honest with yourself and with your staff. If you feature reviews, are they well written? Are they of a reasonable length?
- DO take a hard look at your current site and be brutally honest with yourself. What elements create barriers to service for patrons? What are the pain points that make an action more difficult for users to navigate the site?
- DO conduct research on what web development elements your public might expect you to include, and those elements that are considered passé or no longer effective. Evaluate each one and include or exclude these elements mindfully and with intention. Instead of saying, "We have to have all the things!" ask yourself, "What purpose will this thing serve? Does it honor our organizational mission statement and goals for this project?"
- DON'T plan to include elements from your existing page that are no longer of relevance to your community. You may absolutely love promoting a Website of the Month, but do people actually use it? Again, plan to include or exclude elements mindfully and with intention (we cannot possibly stress this enough).

4

Budget

There is no question about it: your budget will dictate the direction you take with your website redesign. There are "on the cheap" options, and there are extremely expensive options. Rest assured, however, regardless of the number you have to work with, you can create an effective website for your library.

There are essentially three ways you can acquire a new website:

1. Design it yourself, either through a content management system or by coding it all;
2. Contract with a designer/developer to either create a custom site or to select an "out of the box" option;
3. If your library has a newer generation library management system or discovery layer, use the catalog as a website.

Of course, each option has its pros and cons, and we will get into that later on. In this chapter, we are going to discuss budget.

Let us assume that you are either an administrator who is willing to put some money into the project or someone who has enough influence over your administrator to convince that person to earmark money for the project. In either case, you should have a pool of money to aim at this new website. It is no joke to say that if you have the staff members with time to devote to investigation and who have the ability to bend a content management system to their will, you can create a beautiful website with about $600. You read that number right. However, that cost does not represent the staff time involved to learn how to use the content management system you choose, the time to create the content you will feature on the website, and the time you and others in your organization will have to spend meeting in order to agree on what to include, how to include it, and what changes to make. It does not include the staff time

> . . . if you have the staff members with time to devote to investigation and who have the ability to bend a content management system to their will, you can create a beautiful website with about $600.

to conduct usability testing. It does not include the cost of the equipment you will need in order to conduct usability testing, or the cost of the incentives you will probably want to offer to people in order to complete usability testing. It does not include hosting or security or backup costs.

Table 4.1 gives an example of the actual and implied potential costs of creating a basic website, assuming you have someone on staff whom you can pay to self-teach the content management system and you use a solution like WordPress, which is probably the least expensive on the surface.

These numbers are assuming quite a lot. They are assuming that you actually have a staff member who is willing and able, and has the time to devote to becoming your webmaster. We have assumed a salary of $20/hour for a degreed nonmanagement professional. However, we are aware that there are libraries that pay their librarians less. If you are at a library that adheres to a lower salary scale, adjust your costs accordingly. Likewise, we are assuming that you pay your management staff around $30/hour. It could be much higher or lower depending on your salary scale, of course, and again, you should adjust accordingly. This is also assuming an extremely efficient process, involving a short training schedule, a total of two meetings, and a very compact turnaround time for content development and design. It is also assuming absolutely no costs associated with marketing the site to your public or to your staff, which is unlikely, but those costs are extremely difficult to estimate. Can it be done within these parameters? Yes. Especially in a responsive design environment, you can knock out a basic version of your website and just keep making tweaks to it, which you would probably do anyway. However, we would recommend a more generous timeline, which we will talk about later.

Another potentially inexpensive option is to use your library management system, if you have one that enables you to customize content. Since conventional wisdom is that most people simply use library websites to find the hours, location, and catalog, using your online catalog as your web presence is not necessarily a bad idea.

We are not aware of any library that has actually used its library management system as its primary website, although we are sure there must be some out there. SirsiDynix Enterprise's discovery allows administrators to create "rooms" of content that can contain databases, digitized content, and more. We can see this being a reasonable solution for a library that is already utilizing a library management system with these capabilities and that has limited resources, but again, we are unaware of a library that has actually gone in this direction. We do, however, have a very local example of a library system that has used a discovery layer as its website.

Table 4.1 Actual and Implied Costs of Creating a Library Website

Actual Costs		Implied Costs	
WordPress theme (free or premium)	$0–$200	Librarian to learn WordPress basics	$300 (15 hours at $20/hour)
Plug-ins: event calendar, photo rotator, book jackets	$300 (approximately $100 each)	Librarian to search for themes and plug-ins	$300 (see above)
Hosting	Approximately $200/year	Initial meeting with stakeholders to determine content	$160 (assuming the following: 2-hour meeting with head of kids paid at $30/hour, head of adult paid at $30/hour, webmaster paid at $20/hour)
Usability testing laptop	$400 (unless you have one already that you do not mind using for this purpose)	Meeting with stakeholders to approve design	$160 (see above)
Gift cards to offer usability testing subjects	$30 (three $5 gift cards each month for two months)	General work on creating content in adult department (including general library information such as getting a library card and FOIA*)	$800 (assuming a non-manager librarian has been delegated to create the content pending approval and 40 hours of work at $20/hour)
		General work on creating content in kids department	$400 (assuming a non–manager librarian has been delegated to create the content pending approval and 20 hours of work at $20/hour)
		Webmaster to create site, make changes, fix issues	$3,200 (160 hours at $20/hour)
		Librarian to conduct usability testing	$60 (this is for the period of development only, which we are estimating would take two months. This figure represents 3 hours a month at $20/hour)
Total	**$530–$1,130 (would go down a bit after first year)**	**Total**	**$5,380**
	Total actual and implied costs—$5,910–$6,510		

*Freedom of Information Act.

Chicago Public Library contracted with Bibliocommons to revamp its website using a product it offers called BiblioCMS. Traditionally, Bibliocommons was known as a discovery platform that operated as a layer on a library's existing online catalog. Libraries would add this discovery layer if they were unhappy with the library management system's native online catalog or simply wanted a more customized look. Bibliocommons, however, has recently branched out to offer website solutions.

According to an article from the *Chicago Tribune*, the redesign cost the Chicago Public Library system a whopping $1 million (Healy, 2014). Yes, you read that right, too. Of course, the article does not break that number down at all, so it is really impossible to know if that is actual cost for the product and development only, or if that includes an estimate of staff time cost to curate the content for the launch as well. Now, we are going to assume that Bibliocommons has some lower-cost options. We would not write them off without exploring that option if that seems to be something that draws your interest. However, we hope that we have already made the case for not having to spend $1 million on a website in order to have something lovely and functional, and something that you can be proud of.

The final option is to have someone develop and design your site for you. This is probably the most potentially expensive option, setting aside the $1 million Chicago Public Library website. The cost really depends on the content management system the developer uses (open source or proprietary), how much the person will charge for the actual work, how much customization you require and/or need, and whether or not your staff will be able to continue updating the site or if you will need to purchase a maintenance package from the developer.

When we decided to redesign our website, we went with a developer who had a master's in library science and had worked closely with libraries in the past. We spent a bit under $18,000 for our website, just on developer costs. Honestly, this was about what we had expected to spend. We wanted the project to come in under $20,000, and we wanted to work with someone who would be willing to be available to us frequently, as we had a lot of negotiations to engage in with our in-house stakeholders and would require frequent meetings.

Essentially, the "too long; didn't read" of this is that the range of costs for a new website can be anywhere from around $600 to $1 million, with all sorts of stops in between. Determining your budget at the outset will help you determine your direction and your level of customization.

- DO prepare your administrator well in advance of his or her budgeting process. It really is not too early to begin discussing what potential budget you may have up to a year in advance. Doing some homework on libraries in your area that have recently done redesigns is a good place to start. They can give you an idea of their methodology and approximately how much it cost and how much time it took. Administrators like knowing what is coming around the corner when planning for the library's finances.

- DO think carefully about the implications of the direction you think you want to go in when you set your budget.

- DON'T expect to get a web developer or designer who will produce a quality product for $600. That figure pertains specifically to you doing your own development using an open-source content management system like Drupal or WordPress. It is much more likely that you will be spending over $10,000 for a custom website created by a developer.

- DO include estimates of how much staff time will cost. This is an important element in the budgeting process. Even if this figure is not reflected in your budget line item for "web design," if you have to pay hourly staff to perform their usual duties and participate in the website development, the cost will certainly be reflected in your "salaries" line item. Even if you assign salaried staff to work on the website development process, it is a good idea to estimate how much it will cost the organization in their time spent working on this project. This is time they will not have to work on other things.

- DO check out your library management system to see if it is possible to use it as a portal for patrons, especially if you have very little money to budget for the development of a new site. It might not be the perfect solution, but you may at least be able to customize your catalog enough to feature really important things like trustee information. Again, not all library management systems are able to do this, but it is good to have all of your options laid out before you make budgetary decisions.

RESOURCE

Healy, Vikki Ortiz. Library Refashions Its Website. *Chicago Tribune*, April 11, 2014.

5

Timeline

No one wants a project like this to go on forever. It takes a lot of time, and if you do it right, you should be building up interest and excitement among your staff and patrons well in advance of your launch date. Setting up a timeline is essential in maintaining that excitement and helping the staff members who have the most hands-on experience with the project to be able to see the light at the end of the tunnel. However, be prepared for the inevitable.

We are just going to say it. Hardly anyone launches their new website "on time." You need to set a launch date and you need to make every attempt to actually launch on that day, but just forgive yourself right now, because it most likely will not happen. At the last minute, something will stop working, or you will have forgotten to include something that changes your entire menu structure, or someone will figure out that an element isn't rendering properly and you will spend the 24 hours of your launch day scrambling to fix it. Hopefully, you will launch the following day or sometime that week. We launched a few months after our initial target launch date. It is a good idea to do some "disaster" planning and come up with a marketing strategy to address the issue. This does not have to be an elaborate plan. You can cover your bases by having wording ready to post on your current website (if you have one), make signs for service desks and entryways, make "monitor" talkers (small cardstock-quality signs that can be adhered to computer monitors), and come up with some talking points to enable frontline staff to answer the inevitable questions that will arise from patrons. If you do not have to implement the plan, all the better, but it is best to think ahead and have your staff prepped in advance to know what to say if it does happen (and it will).

Now that we have that out of the way, we need to address the broader concept of the timeline itself. If you are fully in control of the development of your new website, you will be able to develop the timeline based on targets that you and your stakeholders set. In fact, to some extent, the timeline will start before you sign a contract, even if you go the outside developer route. If you do contract with an outside developer, they will most likely not want to devote more than a certain period of time to your project and will offer you a potential timeline. You should definitely tell your developer whether or not the suggested timeline is tenable for you and your organization.

There are several things to consider. Will vacations of stakeholders interfere with the completion of the project? Are there other large-scale projects in progress that may require more of your or someone else's time who will be deeply involved with the development and launching of the site? Do you want to time the launch of your site with a particular time of year, event, or publication of your newsletter? How will unexpected, yet unavoidable, stumbling blocks interfere with the timeline? Do your best at the outset to identify anything and everything that may happen to derail or postpone the project, and make sure to have full and open communication with your stakeholders.

It is important to identify all of the milestones of the project and set a reasonable target date. Here are some milestones to consider when establishing your timeline:

- Establishing a budget and determining whether or not your organization will need to issue a request for proposal (RFP) or request for quote (RFQ)
- Identifying and meeting with organizational stakeholders, and selecting your project leader(s) and team
- Environmental scan of design and content options and requirements
- Issuing an RFP or RFQ (if required), evaluating submissions, and selecting your developer
- Meeting of project leaders with developer to discuss needs and wants, and to listen to options and limitations
- Producing content
- Producing images
- Reviewing designs with developer and making changes
- Usability testing (should begin as soon as a rough design is produced to get immediate user feedback)
- Meeting with stakeholders and developer to approve design
- Training for staff who will be updating the website on the selected content management system
- Populating the website with content
- Releasing access to staff members outside of the project team in the organization
- More usability testing
- Producing and releasing marketing pieces to promote the new site
- Testing of site for functionality

- Testing links and proofreading content
- Final round of usability testing
- Soft launch
- Hard launch with promotion

Depending on your budget, who will be developing the site, and your staffing situation, your timeline milestones may look different. The point is to establish one as early as possible and try to stick to it as closely as possible. There will be times when you feel as though the project is going on forever. As long as you can look ahead to that launch date, you will be able to remind people that the time will pass in the blink of an eye.

One mistake we made with our project was that we did not identify our primary stakeholders and decide on our project team as soon as possible. We already had our budget established, had completed our environmental scan, and had our developer selected when we met with staff members who would be expected to contribute to decision making moving forward, produce content, and participate in usability testing. Some staff members ended up feeling slighted or left out of the early stages of the project. They were not wrong. The people who were expected to be on the team had not had an opportunity to conduct their own environmental scans and offer input regarding what they were looking for in the redesign. We ended up with a lot less staff buy-in than was ideal. This made the project go on longer than it should have, as people dragged their heels on producing content, and by the time we did launch, everyone was exhausted, frustrated, and close to being burnt out.

> Keeping stakeholders in the loop with regard to the process and the milestones should help enormously with helping staff become invested and excited in the project.

Again, keeping stakeholders in the loop with regard to the process and the milestones should help enormously with helping staff become invested and excited in the project. You will likely always have some naysayers and a few individuals who make it difficult to reach a consensus, but you are much more likely to have a cohesive, harmonious project team if you begin with being open about the timeline and expectations.

- DO establish a timeline at the outset of your project. This is essential for making sure that you and your team do not expend too much energy on any single element or process.
- DO resign yourself to the fact that you will likely not launch on time. You can mitigate the guilt that you almost certainly will be tempted to feel when this happens by planning for a "soft" launch. You can plan a grand reveal of the new website a month or two away from your soft launch date and this will be when you push a lot of publicity.

- DO have a communication plan in place to prepare for things to go wrong prior to launch. You want to make sure that your team and your patrons understand that you are working out the issues and will update them with a progress report.
- DON'T panic if and when you miss your launch date. Everything will be okay. Just focus on fixing the issues in as timely a manner as possible.
- DO clear your calendar for the week of your "soft" launch to make sure you have time to actively monitor the website and respond to comments from patrons and staff immediately. This is going to take time, and you want to make sure you have that time to dedicate to this process.
- DON'T let your developer completely dictate your timeline. Make sure you convey your needs and concerns and come to a mutual agreement on target dates.
- DO take into consideration potential setbacks like vacations, programs, illness, weddings, and births. Come up with contingency plans and assign pinch hitters for each member of your team.
- DO make sure to check your state's library statute to determine whether or not you will need to issue an RFP or RFQ if you intend to hire a website developer. This process will definitely affect your timeline.
- DO establish your project team immediately. Identify organizational stakeholders. You want everyone to have buy-in at the outset.

6

Understanding What You Want

At this point, you should know what your budget is, and you should have a general idea of when you want your new website to launch. You understand that the timeline needs to include a "discovery" period, during which you brainstorm about content ideas and features you might like to include in your site, and when you spend a not insubstantial amount of time checking out all kinds of websites.

This is really one of the most fun parts of the process, and one of the most important. This is when you get to really look at other websites—as well as your own current one—and think about things like usability, navigation, and esthetics, and when you start envisioning what your website could look like.

ENVIRONMENTAL SCAN

Of course, it is important to specifically evaluate other library websites, public and otherwise. We also encourage you to take the time to evaluate non-library sites that you visit and use on a regular basis. Do you do a lot of online shopping? Take a closer look at your favorite shopping sites and really think about why you like them. Is it simply a matter of liking the products available, or do you also find the discovery options user friendly? How do the sites allow you to limit your search? How easy is it to navigate between options, select or deselect limiters? How easy is it to find information on what the return policies are? Is the font easy to read? Are the links easy to find? Is it a cleaner, more minimalist design, or is it content heavy like Amazon? Is it easy to navigate back to the home page? Where is the menu placement? Do you like where it is? Would you like it better if it were placed somewhere else? How easy is it to find out where the brick-and-mortar location is, if one (or more) exists? How easy is it to find hours of operation or contact information? How do the colors make you feel? Do they excite you, or are they soothing?

Take a closer look at your favorite shopping sites and really think about why you like them.

Do not just stop at shopping sites, either. If you enjoy reading news sites, look at those as well and try to determine what brings you back time and time again, and whether or not it has to do with content, design, or both. Think about your reaction to things like photo rotators and ad spaces (areas of the website that direct your attention to other parts of the site). Are they distracting or helpful? Look at sites like Pinterest, etsy, and Opensky. These sites are currently going for more of an "inspiration board" look, focusing on cards that feature vivid images or graphics rather than text (and obviously the inspiration for Chicago Public Library's new design).

As you engage with this exercise, you may find yourself being surprised at elements of a site that you did not notice before that you find either appealing or annoying. We certainly found this to be the case when we did our searching. We found that we were mostly very drawn to a cleaner look, not necessarily minimalist, but something that gave the impression of wide open space while maintaining a dynamic structure with horizontal navigation. We also realized that many libraries were incorporating elements that perhaps already existed on our website, but these other libraries were presenting them in new, more exciting ways.

Pay close attention to the labels on primary, secondary, and tertiary navigation. Are they intuitive? Is the menu structure itself useful or confusing? In terms of nonlibrary websites, we were very drawn to the searching capabilities of sites like Zappos and Amazon. Pay close attention to where these sites placed features like a search box or logging into one's account. Placement of these elements can be critical to the user experience.

While searching other library websites, become aware of features, services, or elements you may never have considered, but that you find compelling or fun. Consider whether or not you want to incorporate similar features or services when you launch your new site. Make a note of these so that you can address them with your developer.

Fairly quickly, you should be able to identify a few library websites and a couple of nonlibrary websites that you return to over and over because you like the look or appreciate the navigational usability. Amazon and Zappos were the two nonlibrary websites represented on our list. As for library websites, we really liked various elements of the websites of Scottsdale Public Library, Mount Prospect Public Library, and Salt Lake City Public Library. We actually liked all of these sites for very different reasons. We liked the fixed navigation of Mount Prospect's site. We liked the kids page and a lot of the "value-added" features of the Scottsdale site, in particular its "Gimme" engine, which allowed the user to select a genre and the engine would offer a book option the user might like to read (since we redesigned our website, Scottsdale has also gone through a redesign and has apparently disabled the "Gimme" engine). We liked the overall look and feel of the Salt Lake City website. The site features that "wide open spaces" look that we were drawn to and had a visually appealing photo rotator design that featured a summary of what the slide depicted. It seemed fresh, unexpected, and engaging.

When you go through this process, make sure to take careful notes. Be sure to identify where you saw the features that caught your eye and made you sit up and take notice. Trust us, you will get websites mixed up and not remember which features went with which site. Thorough and detailed note taking is absolutely crucial.

CHECKING YOUR SITE

Once you feel that you've done a significant enough "environmental scan" of other websites, take a look at your own site. Just because you're redesigning your website does not mean that you will be jettisoning all of the existing content. Make sure you identify pieces of information you have on your site that your patrons regularly use, and then evaluate those elements to see if you need to keep them as much the same as possible, or repackage them in a way that would make for a better user experience.

Study your statutes so that you know which elements you are legally required to include. For example, in our state—and we are sure that it is similar in others—we have to post certain pieces of information regarding our board of trustees and its activities. We also wanted to beef up our information regarding how the public could utilize the Freedom of Information Act (FOIA), including providing them with an online form as well as our FOIA e-mail address. Strategic placement of this information is important. You do not want to bury it, but you also do not want it to take up valuable top-level real estate.

Similarly, consider how much of your policy manual you want to include. It is clearly important to offer patrons potentially important information regarding library usage, but you do not want to bloat the site with a lot of information that most people would not find particularly useful. In the same vein, it's important to include basic information about your library such as a summary of your history, your current strategic plan, and your mission statement. While many people who visit your site may not ever visit these pages, there can be key moments when it is incredibly useful to point out that all of this information is available on your website.

By the end of this evaluative process, you should have a really solid idea of what design elements you like and which ones you cannot stand, and what kind of content you want to include on your own site. You should also have a decent sketch of the menu structure, although not necessarily the order or labels. Things should still be fairly fluid at this point. You should have plenty of opportunities to change your mind or reevaluate an element or the inclusion of a piece of information. This will all be hashed out in the active design phase.

This was our wish list from our web design project:

- Mobile friendly site, not a mobile site that is different
- NO right-side navigation!
- Must have search box and site map
- Library contact/hours information must be at top
- Vary the logo style—in crayon on kids page, pencil sketched on teen page, etc.
- Incorporate digital history project as tab
- "Request a purchase" feature that generates an e-mail; same for the Friends of the Library page, and so on
- Anything that takes us off site should open a new tab, even Media on Demand
- Functionality to add an online donate/pay feature at some point in the future
- Want a tab that says "calendar"

> You will likely not get everything on your initial wish list. Be able to adapt, to be flexible, and to come to an understanding of what is really vitally important to your organization.

- A virtual tour of the library on the home page
- Interactive Google map with ability to get directions
- Logo always takes you home
- Should be able to navigate anywhere from any page

Some of these items are already outdated or ended up being examples of web design that is considered not so great (different versions of the logo based on age, for example). Some simply turned out to be unimportant (digital history project tab). Some we never got and still want (contact information and address in the header). You will likely not get everything on your initial wish list. Be able to adapt, to be flexible, and to come to an understanding of what is really vitally important to your organization.

- DO make sure to evaluate nonlibrary websites during your environmental scan and discovery phase. Which websites do you personally use on a regular basis? Which websites do you use professionally? Why do you return to them over and over? Think about why your favorite sites position elements the way they do and how that impacts the user experience.
- DON'T overlook the things you dislike about even in your favorite websites. It is easy to find fault with sites we do not enjoy browsing, but there are likely elements of your favorites that have issues as well. Do your best

to identify these (are you suddenly feeling mildly annoyed while using a site? Try to identify why), and make note of them.

- DO make a list of elements you particularly like during your discovery. Ask yourself how each element could potentially enhance and improve your patrons' experiences while interacting with your website.

- DON'T get emotionally attached to a particular element or feature. Bear in mind that you should be extremely editorial when you make decisions on elements to include or exclude. Every element should serve a purpose and the purpose should be to enhance your users' experience, not scratch a nerdy itch on your part (we're looking at you, book recommendation service!)

- DO take careful notes about things you like and things you do not like. Try to record why you did or did not like something. Not only will you want to refer back to these notes during the design phase, but you may also want to revisit your notes throughout the period that you are responsible for the maintenance of the site. The idea here is to do a constant evaluation, and it is important to be able to refresh your memory about why you did or did not include something.

- DON'T skip the step of evaluating your own website. You may feel that you know it backward and forward and that may turn out to be the case, but it is still a good idea to view your current site with an evaluative eye at least one more time.

- DO check your statute to see which elements you are legally required to include.

- DON'T bury things that people are looking for, even if it is not information you particularly want them to have. For example, you may feel compelled to include a list of managers and their e-mail addresses, but that does no one any good if the information is buried. You absolutely have to prioritize some information. Just do your best not to intentionally bury anything.

7

Who Does It?

As established in previous chapters, after you decide to embark on a website redesign project and you have determined your budget, you must then decide who executes the development of the new site. To review, your choices come down to the following:

1. You;
2. Outside developer;
3. Ready-to-launch site.

There are pros and cons to each approach, of course. The important thing is to be committed to your choice you make. Also, remember that by its very nature, your website can and will change. In fact, it must, unless you want it to be outdated again in six months. The point is, even if you come out of the experience wishing you had gone in another direction, you can always resolve to revisit the design in a year or two and plan to have a bigger budget, or more training, or whatever it is you feel you lacked going through it this time around.

YOU

If you decide that your budget and in-house talent mean that developing the site on your own is the best option, the first thing you need to do is decide who on your staff will be the webmaster. This is the person who needs to acquire the most knowledge about how the different pieces of the site fit together in order to keep the site working smoothly, and to be able to make iterative changes along the way. This person needs to be able to learn how to use the content management system you select, needs to have the time now to dedicate to getting the site up and running, and needs to have the time going forward to continue to maintain it, fix it, update the security, and make any fundamental changes as long as you continue to use the same content management system. Of course, this person needs to be on your project team, and should probably be one of the project leads.

The next step is to decide on your content management system. There are some proprietary options out there, but we are going to focus on the two that most people turn to when creating their websites, and they are both open-source options: Drupal and WordPress.

If you ask a room full of people who develop websites for a living—or are even really into the concept of developing websites and have developed their own in their spare time—what their content management system of choice is, chances are most of them will say Drupal. Drupal is an incredibly powerful content management system, and it has an extremely robust user-based support group. These people find ways to improve Drupal's functionality, security, and capabilities. Drupal has a lot of flexibility, which is great for people who want extremely customized websites, or if you want unique features incorporated into your site. If you want a website for your library that will make people sit up and go, "WOW. This is the most amazing library website I've ever seen!" then you may want to consider using Drupal.

Drupal and WordPress work in similar ways. In very simplistic terms, you select a theme, which makes up the base of your website. You then select modules to augment your website with various features and build onto the functionality of your website in that way. When you want to make a change, you need to be able to identify which module is driving the content, identify that module in the content management system, and go from there. In Drupal, each theme and each module is highly customizable. If you are extremely well versed in Drupal language, you would be able to do quite a bit of customization on your own. If you are not, you can contract with a developer to customize a single module and simply do the rest yourself. This is one of the many factors that make Drupal so appealing. You can pick and choose, customize or not, and you have the benefit of a support network at your disposal.

However, all of that functionality comes at a price, even if it is not a monetary one. Drupal can be incredibly difficult for people to learn if they are novices at web development. If you do not understand exactly how one Drupal module affects all of the other Drupal modules you are trying to incorporate into your site, any change you make could affect the functionality of a different module and make it almost impossible to find and fix.

Our website was developed using Drupal. We think our site is lovely; it functions fairly well—and it is like a toddler. You have to watch it constantly. When we contracted with our developer, we were full of naïve bravado and told ourselves that we would be able to learn it with no trouble. Quite honestly, executing a basic update is not that difficult, if you understand databases. It can be confusing to navigate the maze of the content management system in order to find the piece you want to update, and there is a deeper

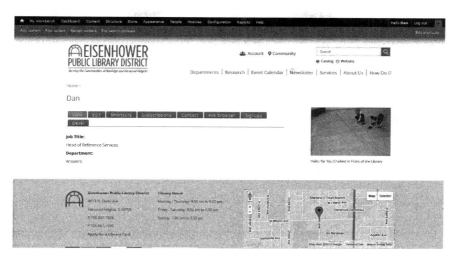

Figure 7.1 Drupal Content Management System

learning curve to acclimating oneself to "Drupal-ese," but once you have been using it for a bit, it is not too bad. Figure 7.1 is a screen capture of the landing page for the Drupal content management system.

The problems occur when we want to change the position of an element or when one of the modules gets updated and we are not aware that it will affect a different module in a way we do not like.

Even when we were still working with the developer, we encountered issues. We had wanted a book jacket carousel. The developer implemented a module that should have worked. For whatever reason, we could never get the carousel to upload batches of records at one time, which was supposed to be one of the nice features. We had the developer work on it, and he was unable to identify the issue. Disappointingly, we had to disable the carousel. We have considered other options, but ultimately made the decision to leave this feature off the site.

In essence, Drupal can be an excellent choice, but make sure you have someone who has the time and tenacity to devote to learning the content management system and who can continue to put a lot of time into maintenance of the site.

WordPress is the other open-source platform that people typically turn to when looking to design a site. As mentioned before, WordPress is usually associated with blogs, and that is definitely a huge piece of the WordPress puzzle. It has also traditionally been viewed as a good platform for someone who has limited web development skills, and that is also true. However, over the past couple of years WordPress has been upping its game with regard to customization capabilities and functionality. It is quickly surpassing the other big open-source option, Joomla.

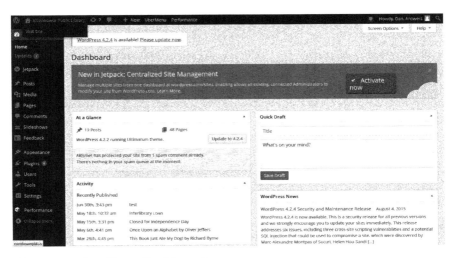

Figure 7.2 WordPress Dashboard

As mentioned, WordPress utilizes the themes-modules model in order to enable website developers to customize their websites. You can opt for free themes and modules, or you can purchase "premium" versions. The costs associated with premium themes and modules are fairly low. As expressed earlier in our cost analysis, you can acquire the themes and modules needed to produce a very functional and lovely website for approximately $500, assuming you do not want to go with strictly free themes and modules. There are, obviously, more expensive options out there, but it is not necessary to spend a lot with this option.

The WordPress content management system is very user friendly. Of course, there is still a learning curve if you have never used it before, but we feel it is much less pronounced than the one associated with Drupal. Figure 7.2 is a screen capture of the WordPress content management system.

WordPress themes and modules are customizable to some degree, but here is where Drupal has the edge over WordPress. Overall, Drupal's components are much more malleable, which can be very appealing to developers who are interested in incorporating a lot of added features to their sites, like recommendation widgets or cost-benefit calculators. You can still opt to pay someone to customize a theme or module, but the return on your investment is really not going to be there in this case.

Our library has opted to essentially reproduce to the best of our ability our current design in WordPress. The developer we used does not offer maintenance contract options, and when we discovered that we would either have to "babysit" the site on our own or find a different developer to contract with for maintenance, we decided to plan our move to WordPress. So far, we have found it to be much more streamlined of a process than we anticipated and while the site will not look exactly the same, most of the elements are similar enough that we feel confident it will look like a new iteration of the same website rather than a completely new design. In addition, our on-site webmaster (who is a professional graphic artist but a self-taught website developer) feels much more comfortable in the WordPress environment than he did in Drupal.

We want to be clear that we are not saying that Drupal is a bad choice. We are saying that it can be the perfect choice for you, as long as you have a webmaster who is confident in his or her ability to maintain the site and make changes to the basic design, or you are willing to contract with an outside developer for regular maintenance. We are also not saying that WordPress is the best choice. It may not be right for you if you want a high level of customization. As we have attempted to do throughout this book, we are presenting your options along with the pros and cons of each decision.

> You should definitely work a period into your timeline where you evaluate whatever content management system is being recommended or considered and determine whether or not it meets your needs.

There is at least one other open-source option, Joomla, which has existed somewhere in between WordPress and Drupal. However, it seems to be losing its market share, as more people become proficient in Drupal and as WordPress becomes more customizable.

These three represent the most well-known and used open-source content management systems. There are proprietary content management systems out there. Some developers will use these instead. The important thing to note about others is that you should definitely work a period into your timeline where you evaluate whatever content management system is being recommended or considered and determine whether or not it meets your needs. Whichever you choose, it should allow you the level of customization and functionality you want while being a system that is accessible to your webmaster.

WHAT IS A WEBMASTER?

Essentially, a webmaster is a person who creates and manages content for your website. This person can be someone on staff or it can be an independent contractor that you pay to maintain your site. Depending on your state requirements, the person you pay to be your webmaster may have an impact in the kind of information you are required to put on your site. In Illinois, if the webmaster is a full-time employee, we are required to post the minutes from each board meeting in addition to the agenda. Essentially, the more hours your webmaster works, the more information you may be required to post. It is all about transparency.

CONTRACTING WITH AN OUTSIDE DEVELOPER

The rules governing how you need to go about hiring an outside developer most likely vary from state to state and from situation to situation. It is extremely important that you find out whether or not you are required by law to issue a request for proposal (RFP) or request for quote (RFQ). If you do not know and the statute is unclear, your library's attorney should be able to tell you (be sure to factor that consultation into your overall costs). This would also be a good time to utilize the hive mind that is the librarian community. In Illinois, our library systems facilitate Listservs that librarians can post questions to and they have proven to be invaluable. You may even get someone to share an RFP or RFQ template, making your job even easier. You can also contact your state's library association or the American Library Association (ALA). ALA has a number of potentially valuable resources available on the website.

Whether or not you are required to issue an RFQ or RFP, ask around to see if anyone really liked—or did not like—the people they worked with through their redesign process. Word of mouth is a great source of information. You can also ask these people questions you would plan to ask referrals provided by the designer.

It may not be important to every library situation, but it is still a good idea to make sure the developer has worked with libraries in the past. No matter how much you want your site to be a reflection of outside-the-library-box thinking, there are certain elements most library websites really do need, like a page devoted to administration and the Freedom of Information Act, a search box to search the library management system, and easily discoverable contact information. Ultimately, you and your staff know your public better than anyone, and it is your responsibility to give them a library website that functions in a way that suits their needs, even if it reflects more updated design or feature philosophies. You definitely want a designer who is going to be open to listening when you have to say, "I know that this is the ideal, but we are required to provide this kind of information."

Once you have an idea of which developers you are seriously considering, make sure you get referrals. Getting positive referrals for someone's work is not a guarantee that you will be happy with the outcome (anyone who has done any hiring or worked in HR knows that this is true), but it might reveal some potential red flags for your organization. Make sure you ask about collaboration, communication style, and follow-through. Also, ask how involved the developer was through launch and whether or not he or she remained responsive postlaunch (there are always issues that need to be resolved after launch, and you may need the developer's help).

> Once you have an idea of which developers you are seriously considering, make sure you get referrals.

There is nothing worse than trying to get in touch with the only person who can fix an issue and having that person be unavailable because he or she has moved on to other projects. Also, ask if the final design the developer produced reflects the needs of the client and whether or not the developer made suggestions along the way.

Check the websites for the libraries or other organizations listed as referrals and see if you actually like them. It is true that a lot of developers will honor the client's requests no matter how esthetically unpleasant, but at the very least the sites should function correctly, and the site will most likely retain at least a little bit of the developer's personality. Also, one of the jobs of the developer is to advise on good design and functionality. You want a developer who is not afraid to tell you when you are wrong, but who will also listen to you when you do not like a design element.

Ask questions about the developer's content management system of choice. Some developers only work with Drupal. Of course, that is okay if you have already decided to either train someone on your staff to maintain the site postlaunch or if you intend to procure a maintenance contract, but if you want to work with someone who will at least consider a different content management system up-front, ask the question.

Take a look at the company's size and structure. Is that a good fit for your organization? If you are bigger and have more stakeholders, you may need to work with a developer who has more time or people to devote to your project. If you are smaller, you may be fine with someone just starting out their own development business, or someone who does not necessarily consider development to be their primary service, but who is willing to do your development as a one-off project.

Check to see if they outsource any elements of the development. Do they work with a designer? Get that person's name and see if you can find examples of his or her work. Do they or can they outsource any module development if you want something the primary developer cannot do or does not want to take the time to do? Again, ask for names and see if you can find examples.

It also helps to work with someone who has a like-minded view of library websites. You are going to become very frustrated very quickly if you work with someone who has a minimalist view of web design, and you are someone who wants to put everything on the front page (if this is the case, you actually may want to listen when the developer advises to scale back, but that is another conversation).

Likewise, make sure that the communication plan is one that you and your team are comfortable with. For example, if the developer wants to utilize collaboration software for all of your interactions but your project leads benefit more from face-to-face meetings, perhaps it is better to find a developer comfortable with the idea of having a weekly Skype conversation and running the rest through Basecamp (or their/your collaboration tool of choice).

Beyond communication conduits (and this might sound a little touchy-feely), it is also a good idea to select a developer with whom you have a positive rapport. It can sometimes be difficult for people who are unfamiliar with industry lingo to express themselves using the "right" words, and this definitely appears to be the case with website development. Find someone who demonstrably understands what you are saying and who is willing to ask for clarification when they are unclear on the direction. Trust us when we say that effective communication when working with someone on a project like this is essential, and it is important that everyone is on the same page, or at least understands where the other pages are throughout the process.

Congratulations! You have just launched your new website. Now what? It is important to have a plan in place, especially when working with an outside developer. At the outset, check to see if there is any type of warrantee or guarantee of functionality, and for how long. If there is not, what are your options regarding postlaunch maintenance contracts?

READY-TO-LAUNCH SITES

Recently, there has been a movement toward a more minimalistic approach to library websites. This may be an obvious backlash to the bloated, text-heavy websites libraries seem to end up with due to trying to push as much content as possible to their users. It makes sense. We are information professionals, and we want to give people as much information as possible. If we assume they will only stay on our home page for 1.5 seconds, then it makes sense to throw as much information as possible at them right away, yes?

It seems very reasonable to make a case for this type of approach, but really what you want to do is offer people the things they actually need from you as quickly and as easily as possible, and make getting to the rest of that information easy for the others who will stick around and hang out for a bit.

The ready-to-launch solutions make this very easy. These are sites that developers have created that are designed to be more plug and play—you add your library-specific content to the template, and you are good to go. These might just be the ticket for those libraries that really need a well-designed but not particularly individual website as quickly as possible. While this book does not include any specific pricing information, these types of websites are marketed as being a great solution for libraries that are smaller and do not necessarily have people in-house who have time or expertise to spend on development or maintenance, so if your library is in this position, contact ready-to-launch providers for pricing information. Because the options are shifting all the time, we have not provided specific contacts for this type of site. Nor do we wish to promote a specific vendor. Anyway, by the time you read this, the landscape could have already changed. Besides, you are librarians and have the skills. Go forth and research!

- DO check references. Don't just rely on an initial meeting or interview.
- DO write a list of questions prior to meeting with a prospective developer. Some potential questions are, What does your postlaunch support include? How many revisions to the proposed design does the fee include? How many in-person meetings are included?
- DON'T rely on what you see on the web as an accurate representation of the person's work. Ask to see examples of original proposals or for the person to explain which elements were changed or insisted on by the client. You never know how much input the client had on what you see.
- DON'T let sentimentality rule your decision. Know someone who is really trying to get their design business off the ground? Let them learn how the business works in the real world. You will not be doing them any favors by "giving" them your business. Even if you don't know them that well, chances are that you are going to inadvertently make things easier on them because you have a prior connection. Do yourself—and them—the courtesy of working with someone only because you really like the work they've done in the past, they have excellent referrals, and your initial meeting reveals an ability to communicate effectively. We guarantee that you'll be disappointed otherwise.
- DO insist on clear and specific answers to your questions. Don't let the person you will potentially be working closely with over the next several months get away with skirting an important issue.
- DO include as many people as possible from project team. Even if everyone on the team won't be working directly with the developer on a regular basis, these are people who will need to have confidence in your ability to advocate on their behalf with the developer. It's a good idea to get their input on whom you'll be working with for the next several months.

8

Anatomy of a Website

The next three chapters address the design phase of your website project. In this chapter we look at all of the "pieces" that make up the pages on a website. These elements are items that you will be making content and design decisions in regards to your website. The following two chapters look at content and design considerations for your site, whether you are designing your website in-house or hiring a contractor, creating a custom design, or using a ready-made website template.

Open the home page for just about any website and what do you see? Typically there is a header at the top containing the organization's name and logo. Often near, or as part of the header, is a search box. Next we come to navigation either at the top or in the sidebar, the main section of the page containing a variety of content items, sidebars, and a footer. Let's take a look at each of these elements in more detail.

HEADER

The header is the top portion of a website that appears on every page of the site, in either the same or a modified variation of what appears on the home page. Your library's name and logo are almost always present in the header, but other information such as your address, phone number, and hours can appear in either the header or the footer. Your website committee will need to make a decision as to where this important information appears. As librarians who were very happy when we found this information at the top of other libraries' home pages, we pushed to have these items appear in the header at the top of our home page. Our developer felt they made the header cluttered and insisted they be included in the footer. He felt sure that people knew to look in the footer for that information if it wasn't in the header. This is a design decision that you will need to make for your

Figure 8.1 Eisenhower Public Library Website Header

own site, and it is better not to duplicate the information in both places. Other items needing possible header placement decisions include the search box and navigation; these items can be placed in the header or on either side of the main content in a sidebar (see Figure 8.1).

> As far as size goes—the bigger and more noticeable the search box is, the better.

SEARCH BOX

Most websites have a search box to help you find the content that you are looking for. A library's website also needs a search box that links to the catalog, allowing patrons to search the collection. The most streamlined way to present both is to include them in one search box with radio buttons or drop-down choices for the catalog and the website. You can also include other search options, such as World Cat, as additional radio choices. The search box should be placed near the top of your webpage as this is the typical place most users look for it. As far as size goes—the bigger and more noticeable the search box is, the better.

NAVIGATION

Navigation is a key piece in both content and design decisions. Website content needs to be arranged in a logical way so that users can easily find what they are looking for. Your navigation, or menu system, is the way they get there. Navigation menus are divided into primary, secondary, and, occasionally, tertiary levels. Primary navigation shows the main sections of your website. The easiest way to envision this is as an outline or the table of contents in a book. You have main topics or chapters (primary level navigation) with subtopics or subheading (secondary level navigation) for each. Occasionally these subtopics can even be broken down into even smaller chunks within those (tertiary level). It is best practice not to go beyond three levels as that makes your menu structure much too confusing for your users.

Navigation leads to a discussion of the hierarchy for the information that you are presenting on your website. Many library websites arrange their menu choices according to the departments that exist within the library: adults, teens, kids, administration, and so on. Underneath, as secondary choices, are things like reading, research, and services for each department. Another common way to structure the menus on your site are by types of resources: collections, databases, downloadables, and others, and then have the

> Try to align your site with users' expectations of where they are going to find something.

secondary navigation break each of those down by whom they are for: adults, teens, kids, seniors, and so on.

There is no best choice here. Your library needs to decide, based on the patrons you serve, what will work best for your community of users. You need to try to align your site with users' expectations of where they are going to find something. Always remember that you are creating your site for your patrons—all patrons with the varying levels of sophistication and expertise—not library professionals. Different variations of your menu structure can be tested out on patrons during the planning stage, before any actual coding is done. With visual mock-ups of your home page menu structure, you can create scenarios and ask patrons under which choice they think the answer would be found. "You are looking to do research on purchasing a new refrigerator. Please take a look at the menu choices on this webpage and describe where you believe you would find the information you are looking for." This way you can begin to understand the thought processes behind the search decisions your patrons are making and see which type of menu structure works best.

Once you have decided and tested the structure for your website navigation, you next need to decide if your menus will be horizontal across the top of the page with drop-downs for the secondary navigation, or vertical in a sidebar on the page with secondary navigation that pulls out to the side. One thing we strongly encourage is that you choose one or the other. Having some choices across the top and additional choices on the sides of a page tends to confuse the user. Also, avoid having the same menu choice in multiple places for the same reason.

SIDEBARS

What is a sidebar? It is the area to the left or right of the main center section of your page. Your first choice regarding sidebars is whether you wish to have any at all. There are websites with a left or right sidebar, websites with both, and websites with no sidebars at all. Some websites, like ours, choose to have no sidebar on their home page, but do have them on the interior pages of the site, sometimes with local section navigation in them (see Figures 8.2 and 8.3). This is a design decision, and there are no right or wrong options here, just the consideration of making information as easy as possible for patrons and other users to find.

MAIN CONTENT AREA

This is the area of the page where the majority of your content resides. It is everything between the header and the footer. The content contained within this area will change for different types of pages. For example, on our home

Figure 8.2 Eisenhower Library Home Page with No Sidebars

page, this area contains a photo rotator that we use to draw attention to major events or information, a section called "Library News" where we place stories about the library, a feed from our calendar showing upcoming events, and blocks at the bottom that we refer to as "ad spaces" (see Figure 8.4). These blocks are used for items that need extra attention or are items that may have their own page for a set period of time but are not part of the permanent menu structure. Your home page should immediately let users know what type of website they have arrived at and what they can do there. Interior pages should have an obvious, prominent page name so that users are aware of where they are within the site.

Items in the main content area should be prioritized by order of importance. Try not to cram too many elements within this area; whitespace is also an important element of design that helps make your page easier to understand. Also consider what will appear "above the fold." While this is a term from newspaper publishing, what it means in this context is what will appear on the users' screen when they open your page—it is what they can see without scrolling. The less scrolling that a user needs to do to find information, the better. Be sure to limit the information on one page in order to limit the amount of scrolling necessary to get to the bottom of the page.

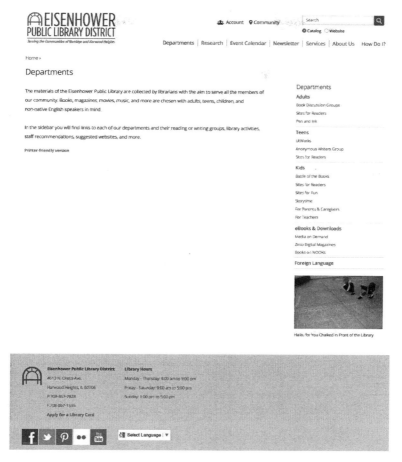

Figure 8.3 Eisenhower Interior Page with Sidebar

The main content areas on our interior pages vary—some are blogs, some are lists of databases, some are full of narrative text, and others list links to outside websites. Content in this center section changes according to the information being presented. Other areas of the page such as the header and footer remain constant throughout the interior pages. The presence or lack of sidebars usually stays the same for the majority of interior pages. Keeping these constant creates continuity throughout your site and makes the site easier for people to use.

> Limit the information on one page in order to limit the amount of scrolling necessary to get to the bottom of the page.

HEADINGS AND HEADLINES

Within the main content area, headers or headlines are used to announce topics and subtopics.

Figure 8.4 Main Content Area of Eisenhower Library's Home Page

People tend to scan a page to find the information they are looking for and headings help them to do so more easily. Headings should be short and clear. Avoid using library jargon such as periodicals for magazines or OPAC instead of catalog, and remember it is best if you can use an adjective–noun combination (Library News, Upcoming Events, etc.). Divide long content sections with subheadings. If a full headline is called for, it should still be relatively short and in the form of a question, statement, or call to action.

FOOTER

The footer is the bottom portion of your page, which may appear on the bottom of every page or only your home page, depending on what you and your

Figure 8.5 Footer of Eisenhower Library Website

website developer decide. If your address, phone number, and hours are not within your header, they definitely need to be in the footer of the home page. Our website's footer also contains our social media icons and a clickable map to get directions to our location (see Figure 8.5). Some sites include information that does not fit within their primary menu structure in the footer, but we chose to include all the information we wanted to present in the top menu structure and not give our patrons multiple places to have to look.

One concern expressed during our development process was if people consider items placed in the footer to be of lesser importance than items found in the header, the main navigation, or a sidebar. You must take this into consideration when adding items to your footer versus placing them in your main navigation structure. While it may be considered standard by some to find certain items in the footer, test to see if items are overlooked when placed there by doing usability testing with your patrons. (Usability testing will be explained in more detail in Chapter 14.)

PHOTOS AND GRAPHICS

While websites at one time were text heavy, websites today are a more visual medium. Photos and/or graphics can be part of almost every website element discussed so far. Your logo is part of your header. Photos are often included in the sidebars or the main content area of pages. You may have a photo rotator on your home page, consisting of a number of images that change at a set interval. You will likely use social media icons somewhere on your site. You may use logos or other graphics for each of your databases or websites that you link to. There are websites that even include photos as part of the main navigation.

> Images help to set the mood of your site, so make sure you aren't presenting stuffy pictures of shelves of reference books if you want to be perceived as friendly, open, and technologically advanced.

Images help to set the mood of your site, so make sure you aren't presenting stuffy pictures of shelves of reference books if you want to be perceived as friendly, open, and technologically advanced. Consider hiring a professional photographer to do a photo shoot at your library.

The images he or she creates will be of better quality and of more use than if you ask a random staff member to take pictures around the library. And make sure your images don't overwhelm your page or push important content off valuable real estate "above the fold," forcing users to scroll to find what they are looking for. When using images, always include very descriptive alt-text for screen readers (more on this when we discuss ADA compliance in Chapter 10).

Now that you are familiar with the common pieces of a webpage, it is time to look at the content and design decisions that will need to be made for your webpages. Content decisions should be considered first, as the content of your site should drive the design of the pages.

- DO take the time to familiarize yourself with all of the elements that make up a webpage before making content and design decisions.
- DO think about item placement of webpage elements based on the importance of those items to your users.

9

Content

Whether it be the sweeping eagle in his flight, or the open apple-blossom, the toiling work-horse, the blithe swan, the branching oak, the winding stream at its base, the drifting clouds, over all the coursing sun, form ever follows function, and this is the law. Where function does not change, form does not change. The granite rocks, the ever-brooding hills, remain for ages; the lightning lives, comes into shape, and dies, in a twinkling.

It is the pervading law of all things organic and inorganic, of all things physical and metaphysical, of all things human and all things superhuman, of all true manifestations of the head, of the heart, of the soul, that the life is recognizable in its expression, that form ever follows function. This is the law.

Louis H. Sullivan,
"The Tall Office Building Artistically Considered,"
Lippincott's Magazine (March 1896): 403–409

Once you have decided your website needs to be redesigned and who is going to be doing the development, it is time to start thinking about content and design. It's very tempting to focus on what the site will look like, but deciding on content should be a higher priority. Louis Sullivan stated that "form ever follows function," and we believe this applies to library websites, where form follows function or design follows content. Your website can have a gorgeous design, but if the necessary content isn't there, then there is no point in redesigning the site because no one will be using it. The opposite is true also—you can have the best content in the world, but if no one can find it because the design is terrible or it just doesn't work, it is also a failure. Content and design go hand in hand, working together to create a great website. In redesigning your website, look at both content and design in depth. This chapter deals with content, both those items that are required or fairly standard for every library website and optional content that you may want to consider including. Chapter 10 addresses a variety of design considerations including

> It's very tempting to focus on what the site will look like, but deciding on content should be a higher priority.

Americans with Disabilities Act compliance, responsive design, branding, and more.

Consider surveying your board, staff, and patrons about your current website to get ideas about what they have noticed is lacking in your site. This survey should focus on site content, not the navigation or design deficiencies of your current site. Ask survey participants about the features they use most or believe are absolutely necessary, and also about the things on the site that they find hard to use. Then ask what additional items they would like to see included on your site. You may find that board members, librarians, library staff, and patrons have some differing opinions on what they use, find absolutely necessary, or would like to see added to your site. When evaluating their suggestions, prioritize what your patrons need and desire as you are creating a site primarily for them. Yes, your staff will be using the site too, but it is your patrons who are the priority.

> When evaluating their suggestions, prioritize what your patrons need and desire as you are creating a site primarily for them.

Earlier in your website redesign process, you did an environmental scan of other library websites and other sites that you regularly use. Now is a good time to revisit those sites and the lists you made and look at the content items that you found appealing. Break down the list items and the items from your surveys as "necessary/required," "would be nice," and "not really necessary." Also, in conjunction with your web developer if you are using one, evaluate the feasibility of each item in terms of cost and time to implement. At the end of this process you should have a good sense of all the content that will be part of your redesigned website.

REQUIRED CONTENT

Libraries are required by law to include certain information within their websites. Other items might not technically be required but are fairly standard among library websites. An example of a mandatory item on our website is the page with the board of trustees' meeting dates and agendas. In accordance with Sunshine Laws and the Open Meetings Act, certain items related to our board of trustees must be made available to the public on our website. Board meeting agendas must be posted on our website 48 hours before the start time of the monthly meeting. Meeting minutes are also posted after they are approved by the board. Required website items vary by the location of your library. Your library director and/or business manager should have more information on specific items that must be included on your website. Examples of standard, although not mandatory, library website items would be information about your location and hours, a link to your catalog, lists of departments with contact information, your mission statement, library service policies, lists of fines and fees, and upcoming programs and events taking place at your library.

NEW SERVICES TO OFFER

The time to start thinking about new services that you may want to offer at your library or through your website is during the early planning phase of your website project. You may also want to consider finding ways to reinvent the on-line services you currently offer utilizing the power of your new website. We used our redesigned website to launch a new program called Book Group in a Bag, creating a webpage for the program that highlighted the book options available for book groups in our community to check out. We highlighted our new Zinio digital magazine service on the new website, and used it as a talking point in our marketing for the new site. In terms of reinventing a service, we created new book recommendation tools on our site with a new online book recommendation service called "I Want a . . ." (this has since been removed from our site because the upkeep was very time consuming) and an on-line form where patrons could ask for personalized book recommendations from our librarians.

> The time to start thinking about new services that you may want to offer at your library or through your website is during the early planning phase of your website project.

With book recommendations being a feature that our patrons enjoyed and asked for more of, we added a number of blogs to our new site. We had blogs for adults, teens, kids, and each of our book discussion groups. The majority of the postings on these blogs are book reviews. Adding content and features such as these that your patrons desire gives them a reason to keep coming back to your site. But to keep them coming back, you do need to create a plan to keep your content fresh. If you decide to add blogs, put together a schedule for posting new content items to them. With dynamic content items such as these blogs, and dynamic items on the home page such as the photo rotator and library news and event feeds, there is always something new for visitors to discover and it gives them reasons to return again and again.

> If you decide to add blogs, put together a schedule for posting new content items to them.

CONTENT MAPPING

Now that you have this huge list of content items to include in your website, you will want to begin to create a content map, grouping like items together. Each grouping should get some type of heading, and each group should be evaluated as to what is missing, what is a necessity, what might be nice to include, and items that most likely will not be included in the new site. You need to evaluate the items on your list to see if they are feasible, and also evaluate your list to assure all required items are included.

How content items are grouped will vary from library to library. You can group items by departments that exist within your library—adults, kids, teens, library services/circulation, administration, and so on. You can group items by resource type and then by audience level—books, online research/databases, downloadables, service policies, and so on. The way in which your committee decides to group your content will begin to form the general direction for how you want your site to be structured.

KEEPING CONTENT DYNAMIC

> Keeping the site fresh and dynamic means that those in charge of that content item's creation or maintenance know up-front what is expected of them.

Be sure to assess how dynamic each content item will be and who will be responsible for its upkeep. Some pages will be populated with content that does not change very frequently, such as your service policies. Some pages will have content that changes yearly, such as a list of the days you are closed for the coming year. Some content will be changed quarterly, or per your newsletter cycle, such as story-time sessions for the upcoming season. And some content will change on a weekly or even daily basis—library news items, upcoming programs, and so on. Keeping the site fresh and dynamic means that those in charge of that content item's creation or maintenance know up-front what is expected of them.

FROM CONTENT TO DESIGN

Once you have settled on the content items that you wish to include and how they are grouped together, it is time to work on the design of the site. This includes navigation design, which will be based on your outline of the site's content structure. Site design includes much more than just designing the navigation and what colors to use, and will be detailed in the next chapter.

- DO survey patrons, staff, and board members about your website.
- DO prioritize patron needs first.
- DO consider adding new services or revamping existing services in conjunction with your library website redesign.
- DON'T make design decisions until after content decisions have been made.
- DO put plans in place to keep content fresh and dynamic, including making sure that staff members know what is expected of them in regard to website content creation.

10

Design

In this chapter you will explore a variety of design considerations. When you evaluated various other websites and made lists of items that you really liked about them, many of these items were probably design related—how things looked or worked—but there are a number of other things to consider when making design decisions.

RESPONSIVE DESIGN

One of your first design decisions is to choose whether you plan to have a full website and a mobile app, or to choose a responsive design for your site that will scale the site to fit all screens—computers, tablets, and mobile phones (see Figure 10.1). We chose to have our site be responsive, thus eliminating the need to design a full website and a mobile app. It also eliminates the need for upkeep of two sites. While some services such as Boopsie make it fairly easy to keep your mobile app up to date, we saw no advantage in having two separate sites, especially with how easily today's content management systems are able to create responsive sites. If you currently have a mobile app that gets a lot of use, you may want to consider keeping it, but if you don't, there is really no reason to design a mobile app while redesigning your website.

Whichever approach you take, when you are doing your prelaunch testing, you will need to test the scalability of your site on a wide variety of devices, both tablets and phones, including iOS, Android, and Windows devices.

> When you are doing your prelaunch testing, you will need to test the scalability of your site on a wide variety of devices.

Figure 10.1 Eisenhower Library Website on a Laptop, Tablet, and Phone

ADA COMPLIANCE AND ACCESSIBILITY

Another design consideration is compliance with the Americans with Disabilities Act (ADA). This requires that individuals with disabilities have equal access to the services that you offer, including your website. Zeldman and Marcotte state in their book *Designing with Web Standards* that Section 508 of the U.S. Rehabilitation Act (www.section508.gov) "requires that many sites accommodate people with disabilities ranging from limited mobility to a vast range of visual impairments, and it spells out what accessible means" (Zeldman & Marcotte 2010, 303). While every library may not be legally required to make its website ADA accessible, it is good practice to try to do this. As Steve Krug says in his book *Don't Make Me Think, Revisited: A Common Sense Approach to Web and Mobile Usability*, "it's the right thing to do" (Krug 2014, 175).

Steps should be taken to ensure that your website works with assistive technologies used by people with disabilities including items such as screen readers or the use of the arrow keys on the keyboard for those who cannot use a mouse. These steps are not difficult to implement and shouldn't result in any large changes to your planned design or add extra expense to the cost of your website; they just require a little extra care when creating your site. Having your site designed to be ADA compliant not only assists those with disabilities using adaptive technologies but also improves the usability of your site for everyone, including those with older technologies and even those viewing your site on mobile devices.

Your web developers should be creating a site that is ADA compliant without you having to specifically tell them to do so, but it is wise to discuss this with them. While some

> Use methods besides color as indicators on your site.

content management systems may be able to automatically check ADA compliance on pages you create, it is good to be aware of some of the website elements this most directly affects.

There are a wide range of visual disabilities that can impact the users of your website. Color blindness, low vision, or total vision loss are just a few of the visual disabilities in which users need special accommodations. For those who are color blind, which can range from the inability to see certain colors to the inability to distinguish color at all, awareness for the colors you use when creating your site makes a huge difference, as does color contrast. Use methods besides color as indicators on your site. For example, underlining and/or bolding hyperlinks within the text gives a clearer indication that something can be done there. Avoid directions in your narrative text such as "click on the green circle for more information" especially if there is more than one colored circle present on your page. Instead add a descriptive link right there in the text. For those with low vision, the simple ability to rescale the text size on your site can make the site usable or unusable to them. The more obvious you make the way for them to do so, the easier it will be for someone with low vision.

For those who use screen readers, whether for low vision or full blindness, there are a number of considerations that come into play. The most important thing to keep in mind in terms of screen readers is that they cannot read images. Any images you add to your website must include captions and descriptive text. When adding images to your site, there is an alt-text image attribute in the coding where you can describe the image. This alternative text, or alt-text, description should be very detailed, as if you were describing it to someone over the phone or in another room, so that they can create the picture in their mind from the words you use. If you were describing the image of this book's cover, you wouldn't simply want to say "cover of the Redesign Your Library Website book"; you would want to say "book cover with the title Redesign Your Library Website in a blue rectangle near the top with computer-related graphics on an aqua square followed by the author names, Stacy Wittmann and Julianne Stam, in a grey rectangle on the bottom." As you can see, the second description paints a much better picture in the user's imagination. Similar descriptive text should also accompany any videos on your site, and it is best to include a descriptive link to a video rather than embedding it within the website.

Any links placed within the text on a page need to be descriptive for similar reasons, so that the person using the screen reader knows what will happen when he or she clicks on the link. Do not use "Click Here" for links, nor the generic "More." The text should clearly indicate to what or where the link is taking the person who clicks on it.

Mobility issues also encompass a wide range, from those with certain limits on their mobility to those who are fully paralyzed. Thought should be given to how this will impact their interactions with your website. To accommodate those who cannot use a mouse, make sure that the arrows

> While it is fine to post documents in PDF form for easy printing, a webpage containing the same information should be created so that it can be read by screen readers.

keys or tab key can get them from place to place on your pages. Make clickable areas, such as your navigation tabs or any buttons you use, as large as possible to make it easier for users to hit the right spot. When listing a book or database title as a link, making the accompanying graphic also a clickable link creates an easier target to click on than a small amount of text is for a user with a disability.

At times you will need to post documents to your site. While it is fine to post documents in PDF form for easy printing, a webpage containing the same information should be created so that it can be read by screen readers or easily enlarged by those needing to do so. A PDF is an image so screen readers cannot read the text it contains. The content you are posting should be available to all users.

> Working to have your site be ADA accessible will help you to draw more web traffic overall.

The best way to ensure ADA compliance is to test the site with the assistive technologies used by those with disabilities. Usability testing with disabled users can be conducted to ensure the site works well for your patrons with disabilities. Testing should be done in multiple browsers to ensure that the accommodations you are including are working properly in all of them.

One last point on making your site accessible for blind users is that it also helps you draw traffic from some of the biggest blind users out there— Google and other search engines like it. Zeldman and Marcotte state that "the more accessible your site is to disabled visitors and nontraditional internet device users, the more available its contents will also be to Google, Bing, and all other crawler-driven search engines" (Zeldman & Marcotte 2010, 318). Working to have your site be ADA accessible will help you to draw more web traffic overall.

NAVIGATION DESIGN

> Navigation is best when it's not noticed at all. (Kalbach 2007, 3)

Navigation is one of the most important components of any website. In his book *Designing Web Navigation*, James Kalbach states, "In order for web sites to be successful, people must be able to navigate effectively" (Kalbach 2007, ix). Steve Krug's take on it: "People won't use your Web site if they can't find their way around it" (Krug 2014, 55). If your users cannot find the contents they are looking for on your site, it is no different than if you had not included that content at all. Web navigation must be clear and unambiguous. It must give the user choices that they know will take them where they want to go. Users shouldn't have to stop and think about what the navigation label means; it should be obvious. "Navigation is best when it's not noticed at all" (Kalbach 2007, 3).

What is navigation? It is a series of hyperlinks taking your users to various places within your website. Kalbach states that it is "all of the links, labels, and other elements that provide access to pages and help people orient themselves while interacting with a given web site" (Kalbach 2007, 5). In designing your navigation, you need to think about how you label your navigation choices at the top (or side) of the page and what will be contained in your drop-down menus from those choices. Navigation should show a user what the choices on where to go are, what they will most likely be able to find in that part of your site, and once they choose it where they are in the site.

The easiest way for users to keep track of where they are on your site is through the use of persistent navigation that is always shown at the top of the page, even as the user scrolls down the content on the page. Making the tab on the menu that they are in stand out from all of the rest of the tabs also helps the users to know where they are within the site.

Navigation labels should be in the language of the patron and be free of library jargon. To find out if the navigation choices you have made regarding labels and placement are clear and unambiguous to your patrons, you should conduct usability testing of those choices once you have mock-ups of your pages showing the navigation.

Once all of your choices have been finalized, you should create a visual site map of your navigation structure. The easiest way to portray a site map is as a flowchart, which can be easily created using software you most likely already have on your computer. This "site map is a representation of your site's structure used for navigation ... provides a top down overview of the site's contents at a glance" (Kalbach 2007, 63). This can be used to see if there is a way to get to everything you plan to include in your site. You can check to see if some items have multiple ways to get to them. This site map should be kept up to date during and after the development process, and can be added as a page to your site with active links to allow users to go directly to where they want on the site.

> No matter where you place your primary navigation, there should be no more than two additional drop-down levels.

Beyond a discussion of the navigation itself, there is also a decision to be made on the look and placement of the navigation on the page. Do you prefer horizontal or vertical navigation? For horizontal navigation, a solid bar across the top or tabs? For vertical navigation, a list of links or boxes/buttons for each, and should they be on the left or right side? We do advise against putting some navigation at the top and some on the sides as this tends to confuse site visitors. No matter where you place your primary navigation, there should be no more than two additional drop-down levels, and we would greatly encourage only having one drop-down level to make the site as easy as possible to use.

You may also want to decide whether or not you plan to include additional navigation options in your footer. Many websites place the links for external items like their social media sites and map in the footer, but you could also put some of your infrequently used navigation options there to free up space on your main menu. Additionally you may have local navigation on interior pages that pertain to just that section. These items are most often placed in a sidebar on those pages.

PAGE DESIGN—WIREFRAMES AND TEMPLATES

A wireframe shows where content items appear on the webpage, most often using a series of boxes to represent each item.

During the development process you should discuss your current site with your web developer. Discuss what you like about it and what you don't like about it. Next show him or her the things that you liked on other websites from your research and send them a list of your favorite library and other websites. We sent our developer the outline of our content structure and the way in which we wanted our groupings represented on the navigation tabs and encourage you to do the same to begin the content conversation. Discuss which items should appear on the home page and where on the page they should appear. Discuss which items are most important and should therefore appear first in the menu structure. After all of this input and discussion, your web developer should come back with a visual representation of what the home page and other pages might look like. These visual representations are called wireframes and can be likened to blueprints for the pages of your website.

A wireframe shows where content items appear on the webpage, most often using a series of boxes to represent each item. For example, at the top of the page will be boxes showing where your logo will be placed, where the search box will be located, and where your navigation bar or tabs will be. Our home page wireframe included the placement of the photo rotator, the calendar feed, the library news feed, and the "ad spaces" boxes. Wireframes should also be created for the various types of pages that will exist on your site—resource list pages, blog pages, and so on. These will become templates for how content is entered into the various types of pages. The purpose of the wireframes at this point in the process is to show a visual representation of items to be included before any actual coding takes place. Making changes to these representations is much easier than making changes once the actual coding has begun.

Early on in the process, wireframes may start out as a simple hand-drawn conceptualization of what goes where on the page. Once agreed upon in theory, you will want to see a more accurate visual representation of what the page will look like. Insist that your web developer provide you with something showing you a mock-up of what your webpages will actually look like before you give your final approval. What you envision one way from simple boxes on a page can look much different once items such as fonts, colors, backgrounds, and images are represented and you see the actual size of the various elements. That's not to say that you can't ask for changes once coding of the site has begun, but your web developer should readily agree that the time it takes to view these created "screenshots" can save a lot of time and hassle down the line.

Once these wireframes exist in their final "screenshot" form, they can be used for some baseline usability testing to get reactions from patrons to your new proposed design. If the mock-up includes accurate representation of your navigation structure, you can even do some testing as to where your users feel they would be likely to find certain items within the menus. This will allow you to test your content groupings and the navigation labels you have assigned to them on your menu structure.

BRANDING

Your library website is not only your online branch, it is also a marketing tool to promote your library in the community and encourage visits to your physical library. Your website should be seen as an integral part of the marketing mix that your library uses to communicate with the public. As a marketing tool, your website needs to reflect your library's brand. The obvious ways in which this should be done would be to include your library's logo and colors as part of the design. The fonts that you choose for your website should also be reflective of the fonts you use in your promotional materials. Be sure the tone of the writing on your website is similar to the tone you use in all of your messaging. If your library is very formal in its communications, use a similar tone on your website. If your library's communications are usually more casual, have the writing for your website reflect that casual vibe. Visitors to your website should be able to immediately see the connection to the other communication pieces that your library produces.

> Your website should be seen as an integral part of the marketing mix that your library uses to communicate with the public.

If your library does not have formal communications or marketing plans in place to follow, invite the person in charge of your library's marketing to become part of your website team (if they aren't already) to assist with decisions related to branding. The writing and communications standards that you create for your website can form a basis for the creation of a communications plan for your library in the future if you don't have one. The rules you set for communications and page creation should be formalized into a style guide to be shared with all staff members working on the creation and upkeep of the site. (More information on creating a style guide can be found in Chapter 11.)

ITERATIVE DESIGN

With iterative design, once you have created your site, you continually make small adjustments, often based on user feedback, to keep the site fresh and current.

Once you have been through a major website redesign project, you will most likely feel that you don't want to have to do it again anytime soon. To make another redesign less likely in your future, or to at least help to put it off as long as possible, consider using the iterative design philosophy in the upkeep of your site. With iterative design, once you have created your site, you continually make small adjustments, often based on user feedback, to keep the site fresh and current. A good example of this is a site like Amazon. Amazon is constantly making small changes to the way its site looks and behaves, rather than doing a complete overhaul of the site all at once. When you come back to the site after such a change you may be vaguely aware that something is slightly different, but the site should work just as well or better and the change shouldn't cause you any additional thought so that you can proceed with your original goal in visiting that site. This is what you want to do with your library website too. As you test different scenarios with your users during your regular usability testing, make (and then test again) small changes in the way things work or look to improve the user experience. Users may or may not be aware of the small changes you are regularly making to your site, but every change you are making should improve the usability of your site and push the need for a major site overhaul farther into the future. Every change you make to the site should be tested to be sure it is an improvement to the usability of the site; this is achieved through usability testing. (More details on conducting usability testing can be found in Chapter 14.)

USER EXPERIENCE DESIGN

User Experience Design (sometimes referred to as UXD or UX) is, according to Steve Krug, "an umbrella term for any activity . . . that contributes to a better experience for the user" (Krug 2014, x). Basically it is everything you, your web committee, and your web developer are doing to make the site as easy to use as possible by making every interaction the user has with the site as effortless it can be. Krug's First Law of Usability states "Don't Make Me Think!" (Krug 2014, 10), and this should be your guiding principle when considering the user experience. He states that you should be making your website easy to use and that things that the user can do on a page should be self-evident, obvious, and self-explanatory (Krug 2014, 11).

To give your patrons a great user experience, begin by following conventions that they have come to expect from websites—for example, clicking on the logo to take them back to the home page, placing your logo in the upper-left corner, or putting the search box at the top of the page. "Web conventions make life easier for users because they don't have to constantly figure out what things are and how they're supposed to work" (Krug 2014, 31). In other words, they don't have to stop and think, they can just do what they came to the site to accomplish. Every decision you make in terms of your website design should be made with the user experience in mind.

- DO consider a responsive design for your new website instead of having a website and a mobile app.
- DO ensure that your website is ADA compliant and accessible to everyone.
- DO carefully plan your navigation and test your choices extensively.
- DO demand wireframes and more fully realized "screenshots" before giving final approval to the design of your webpages.
- DO consider using the iterative design concept for your website where you make continual small changes and upgrades to your website to keep it fresh. This will postpone the need for the next major website overhaul.
- DON'T forget to always keep the user experience in mind at all times to make the site the easiest to use that it can be.

RESOURCES

Kalbach, James. *Designing Web Navigation*. Sebastopol, CA: O'Reilly Media, 2007.

Krug, Steve. *Don't Make Me Think, Revisited: A Common Sense Approach to Web and Mobile Usability*. Berkeley, CA: New Riders, 2014.

Zeldman, Jeffrey, and Ethan Marcotte. *Designing with Web Standards*, 3rd ed. Berkeley, CA: New Riders, 2010.

11

Getting Staff Involved and the Style Guide

Your library's administration and those on your staff with ultimate responsibility for your website (your webmasters) have likely been involved in the decision-making process from the start. The time to bring other staff into the process is as content and design decisions start being made. It's a good idea to form a website committee that begins meeting before launch and continues to meet on a regular permanent basis after launch.

> Your committee must decide who has responsibility for each page on the site.

While it is likely someone on your staff will be charged with ultimate oversight of your new website as webmaster, your committee must decide who has responsibility for each page on the site. This decision affects both who is populating the page during the creation process and who is charged with keeping the page up to date and/or supplying the necessary information to do so. Within your chosen content management system, there are likely differing levels of responsibility that can be assigned to each user. For our library, the head of the reference department and the head of the marketing department have the responsibility of the website in their job descriptions and are considered the webmasters. Our library also has a web and graphics designer charged with the upkeep of the entire site. All of these people, along with the director, have administrative level access to the site with full ability to make any changes they choose. This is not the same type of access that you would give to other staff members. Staff members charged with making changes to specific pages associated with their departments or responsibilities need to be able to access and change those pages but should not have access to be able to create new pages or change menu structures.

Our website committee consists of the director of the library, the head of reference services, the marketing specialist, the web and graphic designer, the head of children's services, the head of library services (circulation), and our young adult/programming librarian. These staff members represent areas of the library that provide content for the website. They can each have members of their department who do the day-to-day updates, but these particular staff members are part of the decision-making body that is the website committee.

All staff members who will be working on the website need to be trained. It's best if this training takes place before you plan to start populating the pages on your website. Our website developer actually came to the library to conduct in-person training sessions on our content management system and the details of our site for staff. This gave staff the ability to try working with the website with his guidance. The training session was recorded to enable staff to go back to review it, or for it to be shown to new staff members as responsibilities changed or new staff were hired. It is highly recommended that your webmaster(s) be fully knowledgeable about the content management system you will be using or take additional classes to become so.

> All staff members who will be working on the website need to be trained.

ESTABLISHING A TIMELINE FOR LAUNCH

Depending on the number of pages that your website consists of and the number of people you have working on it, populating the pages of your website with information could take weeks or even months. As the population of the site's pages begins, reevaluate the launch date you originally set for the launch of your website. Take a look at the time you expect it will take you to fully populate the site, conduct usability testing, and test the responsive design of your new site. Keep in mind that you should be flexible with your expectation of launch and any publicity you plan to do around it. Our actual launch date ended up being months later than we had originally planned. As we got closer to a fully populated site, we decided on a date for a soft launch (without any advance publicity) and to have the site running for a few weeks before doing a full publicity push. This gave us time to work out any issues with the new site before actively marketing the new site to the public.

> As the population of the site's pages begins, reevaluate the launch date you originally set for the launch of your website.

WEBSITE STYLE GUIDE

Form follows function or, in our case, design follows content was the guiding principle in the design of the new Eisenhower Public Library District website. Our new site was designed with a focus on content and site structure first, and then we made design decisions that enhanced the delivery of the content. For staff members to be able to add content to meet our goals, they needed a style guide to follow.

> A style guide helps establish a consistent user experience across your website by providing standards for a uniform presentation of information.

Why is a style guide so important? A style guide helps establish a consistent user experience across your website by providing standards for a uniform presentation of information. It creates consistency across the site along with making sure the site reflects your library's branding on every page. This ensures that the site looks professional, which reflects on the perception of the professionalism of your library. Our style guide reflects the vision that guided the creation of our site—content first.

WRITE A STYLE GUIDE FOR STAFF

- Establishes standards for a uniform presentation of information;
- Ensures consistency across the site;
- Carries out your brand identity on every page;
- Reflects on the professionalism of your library.

The standards and conventions that are outlined in our style guide are not an attempt to stifle creativity among the staff working on the site, but are there to ensure the any new additions to the site work with what already exists and are within our vision of the site's purpose. Our content creation rules and design practices keep all the pages of the site feeling like they are integrated parts of the whole. The goal for those rules and practices is a uniform presentation of information across the site, a site where all the pieces work together.

> Your website should never be an afterthought for it may be your main, or possibly only, means of communication with some of your patrons.

A consistent design flow for information makes a site easier to read, easier to comprehend, and even easier for users to scan for information. And a consistent, uniform presentation of information can make a considerable impact on users' perception of the professionalism of your site and of your library. Remember that this is your online digital branch, and you want to take as much care with how it works and appears as you do with your physical branch. Your website should never be an afterthought for it may be your main, or possibly only, means of communication with some of your patrons.

A uniform presentation of information to the user makes the site:

- easier to read;
- easier to comprehend;
- easier to scan for information.

So what should you include in your style guide? First, include instructions on writing for the web including the conventions that you follow at your institution. The information on your navigation structure and the page layouts you are using throughout the site should be consistent. Information should be included on fonts, heading styles, colors, and photos and graphics. Be sure to explain any custom site tools you have on the site. Also, include information on your web developer, web host, webmaster(s), and website committee. Your usability testing script should also be included.

WRITING FOR THE WEB

> Get rid of half the words on each page, then get rid of half of what's left.
> —Krug's Third Law of Usability,
> Steve Krug, *Don't Make Me Think!*
> *A Common Sense Approach to Web Usability*, 2nd edition

Steve Krug's book *Don't Make Me Think! A Common Sense Approach to Web Usability* is a resource that every web designer needs to have on his or her shelf. While we didn't take his rule literally, we did keep it in mind when we were writing the content for the pages of our website to keep narrative to a minimum. Following are some of the writing guidelines that you might give to the staff working on the website. Feel free to adapt these for use in writing your own style guide.

- Users tend to scan for information, so make the information they are seeking easily found.
- Don't waste space welcoming people to the page.
- Say it in as few words as possible.
- Use short, concise paragraphs.
- White space on the page is good.
- Bulleted lists work well to convey information.
- The first paragraph is most important; it should be brief, clear, and to the point and should engage the user.
- Put the most important information at the top of the page.
- In longer narratives use subheadings; users often skim for information.

- Use headings, short paragraphs, and bulleted lists.
- Name your page clearly so that the subject of the page is obvious.
- Use bold and italics sparingly as they can make text harder to read.
- Do not underline text; on the web, an underline often indicates a hyperlink.
- Do not use all caps; they are harder to read than mixed case.
- Do not use conjunctions if possible in creating a page (they can be used within blog postings, as these are less formal).
- Do not use passive voice.
- Avoid exclamation points!—they make the site look unprofessional (occasional use within a blog post or on children's pages is acceptable).
- Limit or eliminate the use of emoticons, especially when writing for adults.
- Any links that take users outside your site should open in a new window.
- Do not tell users to "use the links on the right"; put the links directly into the text.
- Do not use "click here" or "more"—make links contextual within the sentence.
- Do not use library jargon; use the terms your patrons would use.
- Keep content up to date as out-of-date content reflects poorly on the site; mark your calendar to take down the dated information once the event has occurred.
- Whenever possible, create a new page on the site rather than just adding a PDF.
- When you have finished writing, review what you have written and cut everything you can to keep narrative down to a minimum on most pages.
- Proofread and spell-check before publishing.

WRITING CONVENTIONS

Writing conventions in your style guide can be used by staff in specific situations. See the following sections for spelling, grammar, and punctuation conventions that we chose for our website; these can differ for your site according to conventions used at your institution.

Academic Degrees
- Use capitals and punctuation: B.S., M.B.A., M.L.I.S., Ph.D.
- When referring to degrees using words instead of abbreviations, the words should be lower case—"master of business administration," "master of arts in English."

Committees
- Upper case: Eisenhower Public Library District Board of Trustees, Anniversary Committee.

Dates and Times

- Write the date in full including the day of the week: Thursday, March 7, 2013.
- Only shorten the date to numerical form when naming documents (you cannot use "/" in document names: use 3-14-13, not 3/14/13).

eMedia

- The word "email" should not contain a capital letter or hyphen.
- eBook, eReader, eAudiobook, and eNewsletter should contain a capital letter, small *e*, and no hyphen.
- Try not to use these terms at the beginning of a sentence.

Numbers

- Do not use 1900's; use 1900s.
- Use nineteenth century, twentieth century; do not use 19th century, 20th century.
- For numbers one to nine, always use words.
- For 10 upward, use figures, except when used at the beginning of a sentence ("Twenty-six patrons attended the event").
- Where there is a mixture of the two in the same sentence, use all figures, except at the beginning of a sentence.
- Write out "percent"; do not use "%."
- Write time as 5 p.m. or 10:30 p.m.
- When referring to start and end times for a program, omit the ":00"; write 9–10 a.m. or 1–3:30 p.m.
- Refer to 12:00 p.m. as "noon" and 12:00 a.m. as "midnight."
- Use commas with numbers in the thousands—3,463, not 3463.
- You can use "$" or the word "dollars," but do not use both together.

Organizations

- Capitalize the official names of organizations.
- The proper name of the library is "Eisenhower Public Library District."
- If just using the word "library," it only needs to be capitalized if you are talking about "the Library" to refer to us.

Telephone Numbers

- Do not use parenthesis around the area code: 708-867-7828.
- Do not include managers' direct lines; use only departmental desk lines.

Titles

- Conjunctions and prepositions should not be capitalized in a title.
- Italicize the titles of books, plays, pamphlets, periodicals, films, television programs, and albums/CDs.
- Titles of poems, book chapters, articles, short stories, songs, essays, episodes of a television or radio show, lectures, and works of art should appear in quotes.

Period

- Use at the end of a sentence.
- Use after an abbreviation or title such as Mr., Dr., etc.
- Do not use after headings, subheadings, or in lists.

Comma

- Use a serial comma before the "and" in a set—mysteries, romances, and westerns.

Quotation Marks

- Periods and commas belong inside the quotation marks.
- Question marks and exclamation points belong inside the quotation marks when they are part of the quote.
- Colons and semicolons belong outside the quotation marks.

Miscellaneous

- Use "people with disabilities" instead of "handicapped."
- Use the full name of a state instead of an abbreviation.
- Never have a break in "Eisenhower Public Library District" should the name ever fall on more than one line of type.
- Use "and" instead of "&."

WRITING BOOK REVIEWS

Our website, like many library websites, contains numerous blogs with book reviews, so our style guide included instructions for staff on how they should be written.

- Cover image should be placed to the top left of the review.
- When inserting the image, the width of the image should be 150 pixels; height should adjust automatically (*Note: specific instructions such as this will differ with different content management systems or decisions made by your committee or designer on how images should look*).

- To insert a border to the right and bottom of the image, right click on the image and choose Image Properties, Advanced, and under the Style, the coding should read as: margin-right: 20px; margin-bottom: 10px; width: 150px; float: left.
- Be as detailed as possible in describing the book cover in the alt text for screen readers (example: "Cover image of the book *Beautiful Bastard* featuring a man in a suit adjusting his cuff").
- The cover image should be linked to the item in the catalog.
- Title of the book and author's name should be entered into the "Title" box when creating the blog entry.
- First line of the review should be a direct quote or teaser text to hook the reader, and separated from the body of the review with a return.
- Quotes used should be short and indicative of the tone of the book.
- Do not quote from advance reader copies.
- The review should be two to three paragraphs in length.
- The first full paragraph should be a brief synopsis of the plot with no spoilers.
- The second paragraph should be your review of what you thought of the book, including what you liked or didn't like about it and which patrons would be interested in reading it: "Fans of J. R. Ward and Sherrilyn Kenyon will enjoy this book."
- Add the line "Find (*italicized book title*) in the Library" and link to the item in the catalog.
- Identify the writer of the review by first name and department.
- Add tags using all lower case letters separated by commas.

BOOK REVIEW EXAMPLES FROM EISENHOWER'S STYLE GUIDE

Beautiful Bastard by Christina Lauren

Looking for a well-written alternative to *Fifty Shades of Grey*? Give *Beautiful Bastard* a try.

Chloe Mills is a hard-working intern close to finishing her MBA who loves her job, except for one thing about it, her boss Bennett Ryan. He is exacting and blunt, but Chloe finds him irresistible. And it turns out that he dislikes her but also finds her irresistible. While their animosity is apparent to all in the workplace, in private they can't keep their hands off each other. As their relationship progresses, each must decide what they are willing to lose if the relationship becomes public, or whether the relationship is worth any price.

If you enjoyed the relationship that built over the course of the *Fifty Shades of Grey* trilogy, this book will provide the same rush. This book was also written as fan fiction and previously available online, but it is a much stronger story than *Fifty Shades*. The sexual tension between the two main characters is intense, and all who read it will be anxiously awaiting the next book, *Beautiful Stranger*, which will be out in May of 2013.

Find *Beautiful Bastard* in the Library.

Julie, Marketing

The Beautiful Mystery: A Chief Inspector Gamache Novel by Louise Penny

" 'And a man's foes,' she read out loud, 'shall be they of his own household.' "

Throughout Louise Penny's award-winning mystery series, this Bible verse has been a constant theme, most significantly in *The Beautiful Mystery*. Chief Inspector Gamache and Inspector Jean-Guy Beauvoir travel to a remote monastery populated by an order of monks who escaped the Inquisition and have lived in solitude for hundreds of years in the woods of Quebec, Canada. Gamache and Beauvoir's mission is to solve the murder of the order's choirmaster. With the suspect list limited to the other monks in the monastery, the hunt begins—slowly, painfully, as these men are not accustomed to outsiders. Two even more unexpected and unwelcomed guests heighten the anxiety for the inspectors and the monks, and for good reason. These men are heralds of chaos.

I had a bit of trouble connecting with the book at first, but that quickly changed. The monastic setting really does convey a cloistered feeling, making the characters seem a bit distant. Eventually, I found myself completely sucked into the facets of the central mystery and felt a growing sense of dread for my beloved Gamache and Beauvoir. The ending left me gasping, a little heartbroken, and immediately wanting more.

Find *The Beautiful Mystery* in the Library.

Stacy, Reference Services

PAGE LAYOUTS

Your website will most likely contain a number of different types of pages. Be sure your style guide outlines each of the page layouts you are using. Our website contained a home page, basic informational pages, blog pages, databases and other resource list pages, booklist and pathfinder pages, and pages containing webforms used for collecting information or conducting surveys. Our style guide outlined the wireframe/template for the page, what the page contained, and who was responsible for updating it.

Basic Page

A basic page contains a heading, subheadings (if needed), and narrative. For details on writing for this type of page, please refer to the "Writing for the

Web" section. When creating a basic page, the name of the page should reflect the content of the page you are creating.

Blog Page

Blog entries can be written in a more casual style than basic informational pages on the site. Many of the blog pages on our site contain book reviews. For information on writing book reviews, please see the "Writing Book Reviews" section. Always keep the audience you are writing for in mind when writing blog entries and remember to avoid any library jargon in your postings. All blog postings on our website should be tagged and should list the author of the post by first name and department.

> Blog entries can be written in a more casual style than basic informational pages on the site.

EISENHOWER BLOGS AND TAGS USED

The blogs currently on the site include:

- Library News
- Answers Department Blog: Shelfish
- Teen Blog: "Oh, By the Way"
- Kids World Department Blog: The Scoop
- Local History Blog: "THIStory"
- Adult Book Discussion Blog
- Adult Non-Fiction Book Discussion Blog
- Red Feather Society Romance Book Discussion Blog
- Battle of the Books Blog

Tags used on the blogs include:

- first name of post author (the only tag that should be capitalized)
- adults, teens, kids
- books, audiobooks, movies, music, video games
- fiction, nonfiction
- award winner, classic
- mystery, romance, science fiction, fantasy, western, graphic novel, health, fitness, sports
- biography, cooking, crafts, sports, fitness, politics, history
- readers, picture book, board book

Resource List Page

Resource list pages usually contain a list of databases or websites. These pages can be one or two columns. Each item's title should link to the database or website. If a logo or other graphic is used for each, it should also link to the database or website. A short summary of the database or website should follow each title.

Book List and Pathfinder Pages

Since many of our booklists contain numerous titles, these pages should not contain cover images. List the title and author for each, with the title linking to the item in the catalog. Each title should be followed by a short summary of the item.

Home Page and Newsletter

Both the home page and the newsletter page on our site have a unique layout different from any other pages on the site, and these are to only be updated by the marketing department or webmaster. Our home page contains a photo rotator, feeds from the library news page and the events calendar, and three "ad spaces." The areas that we refer to as ad spaces (see Figure 11.1) are areas on the page that can be used to highlight certain programs, resources, or upcoming events that may need an extra marketing push besides a slide on the photo rotator. Big events that have their own page for a time but are not part of the permanent main navigation menu will be featured in these ad spaces. Our newsletter page contains a digital version of our newsletter and links to past issues that will be uploaded by the web and graphic designer.

Webforms and Surveys

Currently there are a limited number of webforms on our website: "Request a Purchase," "What Do I Read Next?," and "Tell Us Your Library Story." Additional webforms can be created as needed, but we ask that permission be sought first from the webmasters. Before creating any surveys, please consult with the marketing specialist on staff.

Figure 11.1 Ad Spaces

PHOTOS, GRAPHICS, AND VIDEOS

The most important thing to keep in mind regarding photos, graphics, or videos to be added to your website is to be sure that you have the rights to use each item before adding it. In this section of the style guide we specified the image size and border/margin specifications so that all of our images were of a similar size. These details will differ for each content management system and with the decisions your committee has made regarding graphics. We also specified naming conventions (title of book for book covers, descriptive phrases for others) and reminded staff to include alt-text descriptions for screen readers, and that they should be as detailed as possible.

> The most important thing to keep in mind regarding photos, graphics, or videos to be added to your website is to be sure that you have the rights to use each item before adding it.

Photo Rotator

Our home page contains a photo rotator. The photo rotator normally contains four to six images of upcoming events, but can be limited to a single image for important announcements if necessary. The web and graphic designer is charged with creating and updating these images. Staff members are to contact the marketing department if there is a particular event they feel should be highlighted in the photo rotator. Most programs with open enrollment will show up on the photo rotator in the week or two preceding the event. Major events may be highlighted on the photo rotator for a longer period of time.

Ad Spaces on the Home Page

The "ad spaces" on the home page are meant to be changed less often than the items on the photo rotator. Most often these ad spaces will highlight events/pages that do not have a presence in the main navigation structure or major annual events that we want to generate interest in or buzz about. The marketing department makes the decisions as to what items are highlighted in these spaces. Staff members are instructed to contact the marketing department if there is a program or event they wanted highlighted in an ad space.

Videos

Videos are not to be posted directly to our website in keeping with ADA (Americans with Disabilities Act) recommendations. Videos should be uploaded to the library's YouTube channel ("Eisenhower Library") and then the link to the video can be added to the page. Examples of videos that may be added to the site include instructional videos on using the catalog or other services or videos from events that have taken place in the library. If you have a video to be posted to our website or an idea for a video that should be created, please contact the marketing department. Make sure all videos are tagged.

Tags that are used for videos:

- adults, teens, kids
- program
- storytime
- technology instruction
- video book review
- library promotion
- community services

BRANDING ELEMENTS

One of the webmasters for Eisenhower's website is the marketing specialist. If the person responsible for marketing at your library is not a webmaster, consider making that person a part of your website committee. Why should the marketing person be involved in the design, creation, and upkeep of your website? Because the website, while our online digital branch, is also an excellent tool to market the library and its programs. One part of the marketing mix to carefully observe while working with the website is branding. Branding consists of more than just using the library's logo; it also incorporates the colors and fonts that are used throughout the site. By making the staff members aware of the colors and fonts that should be used when creating pages, the pages that they create fit within the site as a whole and within the branding strategy of the library. Following the writing conventions used by the library is also considered part of branding, as it then follows the voice and tone of other library marketing materials.

SITE NAVIGATION STRUCTURE

Your style guide should contain maps of the entire structure of your website for easy staff reference. Begin with your home page and its primary navigation menu choices, and then for each of those menu options, the secondary (and tertiary, if present) navigation structure choices. The easiest way to depict these is by using flowcharts. Be sure to update

> Your style guide should contain maps of the entire structure of your website for easy staff reference.

these in your style guide if any changes are made to your navigation structure, keeping this handy reference as accurate as possible (Figure 11.2).

CUSTOM SITE TOOLS

Any custom site tools, such as bookshelves or a calendar tool, that you have added to your website should be outlined in your style guide. These are not usually items that will be worked on by all staff members, but they should know that these items exist and who is responsible for them. Most library websites include some type of calendar of events, whether it is native to the content management system, a propriety calendar created just for your site, or a link to an outside calendar feed such as Evanced or Google Calendar. Other items are less necessary, but can add something special to your site.

When we created our site, we had hoped to have a number of different bookshelves included on the home page and various other pages, but found that this greatly increased loading times for those pages, so they have been

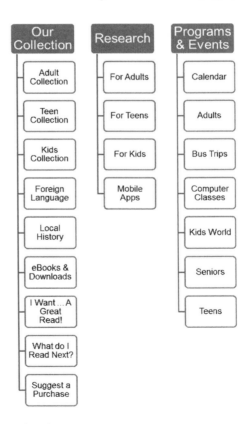

Figure 11.2 Example of Navigation Structure

removed. A library value calculator was included to allow patrons to calculate how much use of the library saved them. This is an excellent tool to include to promote the value that your library brings to the community and all libraries should consider adding it.

Library Value Calculator

Eisenhower's library value calculator is based on the categories and values used by the Illinois State Library (https://www.cyberdriveillinois.com/departments/library/public/libraryvalue_calc.html). The value calculator lists items the library owns that can be checked out (books, periodicals, DVDs, CDs, games, etc.) and services that patrons can use (reference questions answered, computer use, use of meeting rooms, etc.) and assigns a value to each of them. Patrons use the calculator by inserting the number of times they use each in an average month. These numbers are then multiplied by the values to calculate the amount of money a patron is saving by using the library each month. If your state library system does not have its own value calculator for your library to use, a version is available from the American Library Association's website (http://www.ala.org/advocacy/advleg/advocacyuniversity/toolkit/makingthecase/library_calculator).

GENERAL INFORMATION TO INCLUDE

The last section of our style guide contained the names and contact information for the webmasters and website committee members. It also contained information on the content management system we were using, our web developer, and our web host. Instructions were included on reporting issues with the site functionality, and what to do if a staff member or department was considering making major design or content changes.

Reporting Issues or Major Changes

If you find a page on the site that needs adjusting or something on the site that isn't working properly, please notify the webmasters as soon as possible

If you are considering a large-scale change to a section of the website, such as adding a page on a topic that currently does not exist within the site structure or extensively reworking a page on the site, please notify the webmasters before making the change. Major changes to the site need to be reviewed by the website committee before being implemented.

- DO get other staff involved in the website redesign process as early as possible. This gives staff a sense of ownership of the site.
- DO make sure that staff members have been properly trained in the use of your chosen content management system.

- DO keep your expectations for meeting your launch deadline realistic. Periodically reevaluate it and don't publicize the exact date until very close to completion.
- DO create a style guide for staff to follow when creating web content.

RESOURCES

American Library Association Value Calculator (http://www.ala.org/advocacy/adv leg/advocacyuniversity/toolkit/makingthecase/library_calculator).

Communications: Web Writing Style Guide (https://www.hampshire.edu/communications/ web-writing-style-guide).

Create a Website Style Guide (http://www.creativebloq.com/design/create-website -style-guide-6123030).

Designing Style Guides for Brands and Websites (http://www.smashingmagazine.com /2010/07/21/designing-style-guidelines-for-brands-and-websites/).

Develop a Style Guide for Your Site (http://www.sitepoint.com/develop-style-guide -site/).

How to Prepare a Style Guide for Your Website (http://www.wix.com/blog/2010/11/ how-to-prepare-a-style-guide-for-your-website/).

Krug, Steve. *Don't Make Me Think! A Common Sense Approach to Web Usability*, 2nd ed. Berkeley, CA: New Riders, 2006.

Lynch, Patrick J., and Sarah Horton. *Web Style Guide: Basic Design Principles for Creating Web Sites*, 3rd ed. New Haven, CT: Yale University Press, 2008.

Must Have Website Style Guide Content (http://www.collaborint.com/resources/ website_planning/styleguide_content.asp).

10 Essentials to Keep Web Readers Engaged (http://www.ragan.com/Main/Articles/ 10_essentials_to_keep_Web_readers_engaged_45425.aspx).

20 Tips for Writing for the Web (http://www.fatdux.com/blog/2009/08/07/20-tips -for-writing-for-the-web/).

Web Writing Style Guide (http://www.hampshire.edu/web-writing-style-guide.htm).

12

Marketing

We wanted our patrons to see our new site as our "virtual branch" where they could access a terrific amount of information from the comfort of their home, any time of the day or night. We wanted to provide them with the information that they are seeking and surprise them with things that they didn't know were there. We wanted them to see our new website as a source that they could return to again and again for catalog and database access, book reviews and recommendations, or even because they know they can find the village hall's phone number there. We wanted to promise a lot and exceed their expectations by delivering even more. But how did we get them to discover our new virtual branch and how can you drive traffic to your newly redesigned website? The answer is marketing. You need to do marketing to build awareness about your site within your community.

While work is being done on your website itself, work should also begin on the marketing plan for the launch of your new site. It is recommended that your library's marketing person be part of your website committee; but if they aren't a permanent member, they should at least be brought in when you are discussing the branding of the site, the creation of your style guide, and the creation of a marketing plan for the launch of your website. Market research should begin early on in the website planning process with an assessment of the community you are serving. Surveys should be done with patrons on how they use your current site, what they like about it, and what they would like to see changed. Staff and board members should also be surveyed for their input. A closer look at the community on the whole should be taken when making decisions about the site and about the marketing that you will need to do for it.

COMMUNITY DEMOGRAPHICS

You may feel that you know the community you serve. You likely have anecdotal evidence to support some of your assumptions. But formal community

Formal community assessment is critical, and that begins with looking at
the demographics of your community.

assessment is critical, and that begins with looking at the demographics of your community. Demographics can make an impact on what you decide to include or simply what you decide to highlight on your site.

Are there a number of different languages spoken in your community? You will want to make sure that you include translation software such as Google Translate (https://translate.google.com/manager/website/) to allow your site to be translated into a variety of languages for ease of patron use. Does your community contain an aging population? Be sure that the fonts on your site can be scaled to make them easier to read, and think about highlighting certain services that you offer, such as Homebound Delivery or your Large Print Collection, on a prominent place on your site.

The easiest place to find demographics on your community is from government census information. The U.S. Census Bureau makes its census data available online for free at its American FactFinder site (http://factfinder.census.gov/). This site will give you basic information such as the size of the population you serve, housing statistics, age, ethnicity, gender, and education levels of the populace, along with information on country of origin and languages spoken in the home. Do keep in mind that the U.S. census is only done every 10 years. So, if you're in a community that is changing quickly—for example, a town attracting new businesses and the workers and their families who will be moving in to work there—and the census is a few years old, you need to take this into consideration. Another site to take a look at for similar information is City-Data.com (http://www.city-data.com/).

SELECTED DEMOGRAPHIC DATA FOR 60706: NORRIDGE AND HARWOOD HEIGHTS, ILLINOIS

Total population	23,134
Median age	45.1
Total households	9,130
Households with individuals 65 years and over	3,556 (38.9%)
Population with a disability	4,533 (19.6%)

Source: American FactFinder (2010 Census)

Foreign-born population 8,659 (37.2%)

Zip code 60706 compared to state (Illinois) average:

- Median age significantly above state average

- Foreign-born population percentage significantly above state average.

Source: City-Data.com

COMMUNITY PSYCHOMETRICS

> Psychometrics looks at consumer behavior—what a person does and enjoys, not just who they are and where they live.

Besides demographics, another way to look at the community you are serving with your website is to look at community psychometrics. Psychometrics takes into account more than just demographic characteristics of your population. Psychometrics looks at consumer behavior—what a person does and enjoys, not just who they are and where they live. If your library does not subscribe to a service that provides this information, you can get free information on the top lifestyle segments in your community through Nielson's MyBestSegments website (http://www.claritas.com/MyBestSegments/Default.jsp?ID=20). By inputting the zip code of the community that you serve, you can get a listing of the five most common lifestyle segments in your area. This information is provided in alphabetic, not predominance, order, but for those libraries not able to afford to subscribe to this or a similar service, it can give you some details about members of the most common lifestyle groupings in your community. Our library did not subscribe to a service that provided this type of information when we launched our website, so the information from the MyBestSegments website was one of the inputs we used in planning our marketing strategy.

Nielson has three different segmentation systems on the site: PRIZM, P$YCLE, and ConneXions. PRIZM deals with a wide variety of consumer behaviors; P$YCLE deals with financial, spending, and investment decisions; and ConneXions deals with communications and technology behaviors. All three include demographic information in their segmentation systems. In looking at these in terms of our website, we decided PRIZM and ConneXions segmentation were most applicable to find out more about the community that we serve in relation to our website launch.

Our top five PRIZM segments for the community that we serve included three mature/older groups, one young group without children, and one middle-aged group with children. This went along with the anecdotal and census information showing a slightly older demographic in our service population. But the segmentation that gave us some cause for concern in launching our new website was the ConneXions segments. With names like Antenna Land, Dial-up Duos, Early-Bird TV, Opting Out, and Tech Skeptics, these segments showed a population who weren't technologically savvy and who probably wouldn't be very excited that we were updating our website. We realized that we were going to be marketing our new website to a population that contained a fair number of technophobes and/or late technology adopters.

How do you market a new website to patrons who may or may not care about your website? How do you get them excited about great new features that they may not seek out on their own? Instead of just telling them about the new features, we decided we needed to be out in the community, demonstrating all that our new website could do for them. We created a marketing plan based around this idea.

CREATING A MARKETING PLAN FOR YOUR WEBSITE

Once you have done some formal research about the community that your library and your new website are serving, it is time to create a marketing plan. Begin by deciding on your goals and objectives. What are your main goals? They are most likely to create awareness of the redesign and to drive traffic to your site. You want your community to be aware that your site exists, aware that it has been redesigned, and aware of all the useful new and improved features that exist on the site. You also want to get people to go to the site and try it out for themselves. Having the website generate new visits to your library and new library card sign-ups can also be considered goals for your plan.

Deciding how you are going to market your new site comes next. We created a branding statement for the entire website marketing campaign, "Eisenhower 24/7," which appeared on all materials associated with the launch of our website. Colors for this campaign were similar to the colors we were using throughout the library and on our website at that time during our anniversary year in 2013. (We have since switched our logo and branding colors away from the maroon and blue/gray we used at the time to green and a bronze-y brown.) We created messaging to go along with the launch of the new website as our "online branch, available twenty-four hours a day, seven days a week" and touting some of its convenient new features. We planned publicity and promotions, including giveaways. We also strategized to find as many opportunities as possible to be out in the community, demonstrating the features of our new website. A copy of Eisenhower library's marketing plan for the website is included in Appendix.

DEMOS OF THE SITE OUT IN THE COMMUNITY

Find as many opportunities to demonstrate your website to community members as possible. Consider taking a three-prong approach to this. First, use passive marketing with signage, encouraging patrons to ask for a demonstration of the features they are interested in learning more about. Second, set up a table in the lobby of the library on a regular basis while the site is new to demonstrate the website and what it can do, and to give patrons a very visible place to stop by and ask questions about it. Third, get outside the library to talk to community members who may not be regular visitors to the library building. If you can, bring along a mobile hotspot and a laptop and/or iPad to do live demonstrations. Go to your local community carnival, to local farmers markets, to your legislative district fair, and to senior fairs. If your community doesn't have these types of events and opportunities, consider creating your own by asking the local grocery store, mall, or other busy place in your town if you can set up your tent or table there. Find ways to go to where your community members are.

TALKING POINTS: WHAT TO HIGHLIGHT ABOUT YOUR NEW SITE

Use what you know about your community as a framework for creating conversation talking points to give to your staff who will be manning your table at community events.

Use what you know about your community as a framework for creating conversation talking points to give to your staff who will be manning your table at community events. You will want to highlight any improvements you made to your site and any new features the site has to offer. You may also want to highlight features that may have always been part of what your library has to offer that are now easier to find or use on the new site.

Tailor your message to the event you are at. If you are at the local carnival talking to kids and parents, show off the kids' section of your site and any new features that would appeal to kids and parents such as TumbleBooks (online e-books for kids). If you are at the local senior center, highlight the fact that the fonts on the site can be enlarged and talk about how they can sign up online for your home delivery service. By finding the particular features of your library and your library's website that appeal to a person, you are more likely to get them to visit the site and/or your library. Our research into our community's psychometrics had revealed that many people in our top segments were magazine subscribers. By highlighting and demonstrating our new digital magazine service (Zinio) on the new site, we had many people excited that they could download digital copies of the magazines they liked to read for free from our website. This led to them being excited to go to our new website and got some people to sign up for new library cards so that they could use the service. We even had people come back to us at other events and thank us for demonstrating it to them and tell us how much they enjoyed it.

GIVEAWAYS

Everybody likes free stuff. Plan to have branded giveaways to hand out at the events you attend. The items we had created were branded with the "Eisenhower 24/7" logo of the marketing campaign, and also included our website address.

We created three different informational bookmarks and had them professionally printed. There was one for adults, one for teens, and one for kids; each of them touted features of the site that would appeal to those age groups (see Figure 12.1). The backs of all three bookmarks were the same, with links to the home page, the adult collection page, the teen collection page, and the kids' collection page.

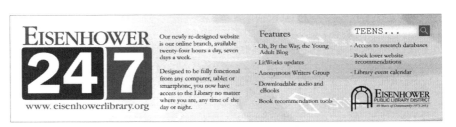

Figure 12.1 "Eisenhower 24/7" Bookmarks

Figure 12.2 "Eisenhower 24/7" Microfiber Screen Cleaner

Our other giveaway was a microfiber screen cleaner (see Figure 12.2) that you could stick to the back of your phone or device. It had the logo and our website address. What better way to market your website than on something that the recipients had with them all the time? If buying give-aways is not currently part of your job, look to your marketing and/or out-reach staff within your library for assistance in finding such items. If no one in your library currently deals with such items and you find you are tasked with the job, a simple web search for imprinted items should lead you to companies that can produce such merchandise. Your local chamber of commerce is also an excellent resource, as there may be companies in your community that do this.

RECRUITING USABILITY TESTING PARTICIPANTS

Talking to members of the community about your new website gives you the perfect opportunity to recruit participants for your ongoing usability testing. We found this to be especially true of the times when we had a table set up in the lobby of the library. We included a sign on our table asking people if they wanted to help us improve our website. Once we began talking to people, some would ask us about the sign; others we recruited. When we were in the library, one of us simply left the table with that person and did the usability testing in another room. If we were outside the library, we took their information and set up a time convenient to them to have them participate. (You'll find more on conducting usability testing in Chapter 14.)

> Talking to members of the community about your new website gives you the perfect opportunity to recruit participants for your ongoing usability testing.

While you may have never considered that marketing would become part of your job when you took on the redesign of your website, it should now be evident that you need to know your community to know how to design content for your website, to decide on which items to highlight, and to figure out how to get them excited about your website. The talking points you create to "sell" the website to them and the excitement that you build about the launch of your site can make a huge difference in the perception of the success of your new redesign. Getting out in the community to talk about your site and get feedback on it will keep the site fresh and current into the future.

- DON'T forget to include your library's staff member in charge of marketing on your website committee, especially as you plan your website launch details.
- DO look at your community's demographics and psychographics when making decisions regarding your website and its promotion to your community.
- DO create a marketing plan for your website to inform your patrons and your community of the benefits of the new site.
- DO get out in the community and demonstrate how your website works.
- DO create talking points for staff members about the unique features of your website.
- DO plan for promotional giveaways if your budget allows.
- DO recruit usability testing participants while you are out in the community.

13

Launch

By giving your stakeholders a window of time for launch ("late spring") rather than an exact date, you will build in some flexibility in case things don't go as smoothly or as quickly as you would like.

You have put so much work into convincing stakeholders of the need for a redesigned website. You have conducted your search for a web developer or made the decision to do the work in-house. You have surveyed other sites, created lists of desired features, and made decisions on what content should be part of your site and how the navigation should look. You have created a website committee, gotten staff buy-in, and worked hard to populate your site with the necessary content. You have done prelaunch testing of the site to assure that it works the way it should. It is now time to launch the site for public use.

The first thing to remember is that there is a chance your website may not launch on your originally anticipated date. Realize that you need to consider your timeline to be fluid. It may take longer than expected to populate all your pages. Your prelaunch testing may find items that need to be corrected before the site goes live. Our launch was delayed by a number of months for a variety of issues. By giving your stakeholders a window of time for launch ("late spring") rather than an exact date, you will build in some flexibility in case things don't go as smoothly or as quickly as you would like.

TEST YOUR RESPONSIVE DESIGN

One thing you need to make sure you do before launch is to test your site in a variety of browsers and on many different types and sizes of mobile devices, tablets, and phones. Your site may look beautiful and work perfectly in Firefox and Chrome, but try opening it in Internet Explorer and suddenly you have problems. The same thing can happen on mobile devices. Your responsive design may be scaling perfectly on that tablet, but when you try to open it on a mobile phone, suddenly you have no menu. It may work as it is supposed to on an iPhone but not on an Android phone or vice versa. Be sure to discuss with your web developer who is responsible for this testing before launch so that you are not scrambling after launch to figure out why you have patrons reporting missing menus or other problems.

Once you are sure that your site is working well in all browsers and on all devices, and you have tested the site using real-life scenarios during prelaunch usability testing, you are ready to go live. Eisenhower library used a three-step launch strategy with an unannounced soft launch, a time for issue resolution and comment response, followed by a hard launch with full promotional pitch.

SOFT LAUNCH

> On launch day, you will want your marketing and communications staff members to be fully prepared for go-live with informational signage.

Eisenhower Public Library District's newly redesigned website was launched with little advance warning to the public. Staff members knew the go-live date and were ready, but the public simply knew it was coming, turned on their computers one day in early May 2013, and our website had a totally different look. See Figure 13.1 to view the difference between our old site and how the new site looked on launch day.

On launch day, you will want your marketing and communications staff members to be fully prepared for go-live with informational signage. You will want front-end service staff members prepared with talking points about the website and have them able to assist patrons who have problems. We had signs on every computer in the library announcing the change and telling patrons how to ask for assistance or report any issues. Announcement signs were placed on the doors to the library and information about our new website was added to the monitor in the lobby (see Figure 13.2). The home page of the website itself had an announcement on the photo rotator and a library news item with full information on the new website redesign. Both the photo rotator slide and the news story had a link to a form that patrons could fill out in case they had comments or questions. Be sure to meet with your marketing staff before launch to iron out details regarding signage.

RESPONDING TO COMMENTS

I don't like your new website. The old website was easier to use and understand. Please go back.

Website Feedback
May 7, 2013

Figure 13.1A Eisenhower Library Website Prelaunch

Isn't this one of our fears when redesigning a website? That no matter how much you test it and try to make it the best it can be, your patrons are going to dislike it when it launches? You are going to get feedback on your new website, both positive and negative, and you need to prepare for it. Since we knew we were going to get comments from our patrons, we wanted to make it as easy as possible for them to get their comments to us and to make sure these comments got to us in a timely manner. And when you ask for feedback, you need to be prepared to respond to it when it comes in, even when it is like the comment above.

The feedback we received in those first few weeks after launch fell into three broad categories. About a third of the feedback we received were positive comments and compliments on the change, telling us the new website was "fantastic" "streamlined and pretty" and "excellent and long overdue." We responded to each of these comments and thanked them for taking the time to let us know their thoughts. About a third were issues and problems that people were encountering; these were things that had to be corrected immediately. We tried to fix the problems ourselves as soon as we were notified or let our web developer know of the situation if it wasn't something that we could fix ourselves. We responded to these comments by letting them know the status of the issue

Figure 13.1B Eisenhower Library Website on Launch Day

and thanking them for letting us know about it. If it wasn't something that could be fixed immediately, we followed up with them once the issue was resolved. We occasionally had to ask these patrons for more details on the issue to get the item resolved. The last third of our comments were from people who needed a little reassurance and hand-holding, and we let them know that everything would be okay with this change that they were not convinced was for the best (such as the comment above). These were often vague statements such as "hard to search on," "not as convenient," "difficult to find what I need," "sorry to write to you, I am a senior citizen so not so savvy." We responded to these people by asking them exactly what they were trying to do or having trouble with.

Figure 13.2 Lobby Monitor Announcement

We explained how to do the things they wanted to do and offered to sit down with them one-on-one at the library to show them. Most of these people became much happier with the new website once they were shown how it worked and that they could do the same things they had always done on the old site.

The most important thing to remember in asking for feedback is that you need to be ready to respond to it, no matter what it is. We responded to every comment or concern we received. We thanked people for the positive comments, thanked them for pointing out issues and kept them up to date on the status of the problem, or reassured people on how to do things on the new site when they were concerned about the change.

> The most important thing to remember in asking for feedback is that you need to be ready to respond to it, no matter what it is.

About a third of our comments in the first hours, days, and weeks after launch were actual issues with the website that needed to be addressed. Once you launch your website, you shouldn't assume that everything is going to work perfectly. Things are going to go wrong no matter how diligently you tested the site before launch. You just need to be prepared. Have your web developer and committee on standby on launch day and aware that they may be called upon when problems arise. Issues are to be expected, but quick resolutions should also be expected. Be sure that you have spelled out in your contract with your web developer your expectations for support on launch day and the weeks immediately following so that he or she does not move on to new projects considering yours to be complete.

Keep track of these issues as they arise. These are excellent testing scenarios for your next round of usability testing. Make changes to get the problems fixed and then test those changes to be sure they are making the website work better, not causing additional issues. Consider recruiting those who have taken the time to contact you as participants in future usability testing.

HARD LAUNCH WITH FULL MARKETING PUSH

Once you have your website up and running, have had patrons and staff using it for a few weeks, and have corrected any issues that have arisen, you are ready for a full marketing push, a hard launch. With an early May soft launch, we had planned for a full rollout of the site approximately one month later in early June. We contacted the local paper to do a story on the new website and its features. We set up a table in the lobby to promote the new features of the site. And we took every opportunity to get out in the community and tell the public about our new website and all it could do.

Following the strategy laid out in our marketing plan, we were intent on showing the public what the website could do rather than just telling them. We had special giveaways created for use in conjunction with the website launch. Bookmarks were created for adults, for teens, and for kids touting special website features that would appeal to each group. We also had as giveaways the microfiber screen cleaners that could be stuck to the back of a phone or tablet and that kept our web address right there in our patrons' hands at all times on devices they would be using to access the site.

The microfiber screen cleaners were a huge hit with the public and gave us the perfect opportunity to get people into a discussion about our new website. When people approached us to ask how they could get "one of those screen cleaner things," we would say "All you have to do is listen to us tell you about our new website!" By asking them a few key questions (where they lived, what they usually did at the library, what they used the website for), we were able to concentrate on key features of the new site that would be of interest to them We also launched our new Zinio digital magazine service at the same time as the new site, and many people we spoke with were very excited about the new service. Excitement about our new site and services led to a number of new library card applications because people wanted to be able to use the new services we were providing.

It should now be obvious that launch isn't simply turning on the new website when it is finished. You should have a well-thought-out plan that encompasses a marketing plan, signage and communication on launch day, and feedback and response channels. Having a plan for how to deal with the inevitable glitches that will happen and having the staff on hand to answer questions and offer assistance will make the launch of your new website a much easier process.

LAUNCH CHECKLIST

- Completed website
- Completed prelaunch usability testing
- Completed responsive design testing in a variety of browsers and on a variety of devices
- Website marketing plan
- Signage
- Feedback channels for patron comments and questions
- Extra staff
- Web developer on site (or available by phone)
- Talking points for staff
- List of community events to attend
- Promotional giveaways

- DO test your responsive design in a variety of browsers and on different types of mobile devices.
- DO plan a soft launch to work out any issues that may crop up.
- DO talk to your web developer so that he or she is available on launch day to handle problems as they arise.
- DO plan to respond to all comments that you receive regarding your website.
- DO promote your new website in your community.

14

Postlaunch and Usability Testing

One of the most important factors in deciding to use iterative design for our website was that we wanted to keep the content current and the site fresh, thus eliminating the need for a total overhaul and redesign every few years. By making small changes on a regular basis based on how your patrons use your site, you keep it working well for their desired uses.

Be sure your website committee continues to meet after your site has been launched. While the meetings can become less frequent, it is still a good idea to meet on at least a quarterly basis. During these meetings, discussions should take place on suggested updates to the site, problems encountered, suggestions or comments made by staff or patrons regarding the website, reports on usability testing, and reports on any website analytics. Any reports on ongoing support from your web developer or web host should also be shared by the webmaster(s).

When you originally signed your contract with your web developer, decisions should have been made regarding web hosting and continued support. You will likely have signed some type of maintenance contract with your web developer and have a yearly contract for web hosting. These should be evaluated by your committee every time they come due to see if any changes need to be made.

USABILITY TESTING

The best way to keep your site current is to conduct ongoing usability testing. What is usability testing? According to Steve Krug in his book *Rocket Surgery Made Easy: The Do-It-Yourself Guide to Finding and Fixing Usability Problems*, usability testing is watching people try to use your website with the intention of making it easier to use or proving that it is easy to use (Krug 2010, 13). You are not just asking people what they think about the site you created or redesigned; you will actually be watching them use it after giving them specific tasks. We did the tests with three to five people per testing cycle, and gave each of them the same three or four scenarios to perform.

Why do usability testing? Usability testing gives you a chance to interact with users of your website, get their honest feedback, and use their input to make your website better. Usability testing should be done on a regular basis to catch any problems that might occur and to test any iterative design changes that you make to your website. Our goal has been to conduct usability testing monthly.

> Usability testing gives you a chance to interact with users of your website, get their honest feedback, and use their input to make your website better

Usability testing should begin before launch of your site to help you catch any problems you may have overlooked. For us, prelaunch usability testing with staff helped us to catch the fact that we had failed to put an account log-in link on the home page. We also tested the site whenever we made changes to make sure that what we had done made the site easier for patrons to use.

You can conduct usability testing without buying any extra equipment, but we do recommend getting your hands on a copy of Steve Krug's book. It contains a great deal of useful information and a script that you can tailor to your needs. The usability testing procedures and script that we used are adapted from this book. Krug calls his book "a complete teach-yourself-how-to-do-it guide" (Krug 2010, 10) to usability testing, and we have definitely found that to be true. You can find a copy of his usability testing script on his book's companion website *Advanced Common Sense* (https://www.sensible.com/downloads-rsme.html).

If you do have money to spend, consider getting a screen recording program such as Camtasia, which records what is happening on the screen and also the participants' voices. This allows the person conducting the test to concentrate on what the patron is doing and saying instead of taking notes while the test is in progress. Our marketing department has a laptop dedicated to usability testing with Camtasia software on it. The laptop is also used for outreach at events.

> You might be surprised at how easy it is to get people to participate in usability testing.

You might be surprised at how easy it is to get people to participate in usability testing. One way to increase participation is by offering a small gift for taking part in the test. We set up a table in the library's lobby with a sign asking them to help us improve our website (see Figure 14.1). Some people stopped by; some we stopped and asked to participate. We offered inexpensive incentives ($5 gift certificates to our café or a library T-shirt) to motivate people to help us. We also assured them that it would take no more than 15 minutes of their time. Usability testing, even with a small incentive for each person, cost us very little—three to five people per month times a $5 incentive equals a bargain for the useful information that it provided to us.

Ask Us How

You Can Help Us

Improve Our Website

Figure 14.1 Usability Testing Recruitment Sign

Following a procedure similar to what Krug outlines in his book, we began the testing by reassuring our participants that they could not do anything wrong, that we were asking them to test the website, and that we were not testing them. We assured them that we wanted to hear their honest opinions on the way it worked. We then asked them some simple questions: where they lived, if they had a library card, how often they came to the library, and if they had used our website before. Next we had them take a look at the home page of our site and tell us what they thought of it and what they thought they could do there. Then we had them attempt to use the website to do three assigned tasks. We turned the tasks we wanted our participants to accomplish into detailed scenarios. These were like small stories telling them what their character wanted to do on the website and even why they would be attempting that task. Krug likens these exercises to what you might give to actors during an improvisational exercise with their character and motivations (Krug 2010, 53). The participants are asked to perform these tasks and to think aloud while they are doing them, explaining why they are making the choices they are on your website. This will help you to understand the reasoning behind the things they decide to do and why they make certain menu choices or click on certain links. Refrain from interfering or offering helpful hints. If they forget to think aloud, you can remind them and ask them to explain why they did what they did.

This process is part of the iterative design of our website where we test, make changes, and then test again. When our testing scenarios uncovered problems or issues with the website, these were immediately addressed if they were critical, or brought before the website committee if they could wait to be discussed. Once these issues were rectified, the same scenarios were run again to see if what had been done had corrected the problem.

Testing scenarios were usually decided upon during website committee meetings or by the webmasters. Any department or staff member could make suggestions for items to test. Usability testing is most often run with adults as the participants, but can be run with children or teens to test out certain aspects of the site that they would be using. Testing with children can be tricky, especially with those who are just learning to read, but can be done. Testing should also be considered with disabled patrons to see if any issues arise in their use of the site.

Here are a few examples of scenarios we asked participants to try, why we decided to test those things, and what we found out from each.

USABILITY TESTING SCENARIO ONE

On your last library visit you checked out five books. You only had time to read three of them and would like to renew the other two. How do you sign into your account to renew your books?

This was one of the first scenarios we tried out before launch to make sure that it was easy for patrons to sign into their library accounts. Luckily we tried this out with staff first because we found that we had failed to put an account log-in box anywhere on the home page when we were designing our site. We also noticed that most subjects looked to the top right corner for this sign-in box. By taking a quick look at some websites, we realized this was a fairly standard location for this type of account log-in, so that was where we added it to the site. This correction was made before launch and the scenario was run again with patrons after launch.

USABILITY TESTING SCENARIO TWO

You just got home from the library and were impressed with how helpful one of the staff members in the answers (adult reference) department was when you were there. You would like to let his or her manager know about the excellent service you received. How do you find the contact information for the department manager?

We found out that our test subjects struggled with this request and that our contact information for the library departments was very difficult to find. To solve this we moved departmental contact information from where it was located to a new location based on where patrons had been looking for it. We then ran the same testing scenario again to be sure that the information was easier to find.

USABILITY TESTING SCENARIO THREE

You are new to the area and would like to apply for a library card online. How would you go about doing this?

This scenario was created because our library services department told us that online library card applications had dropped in the months after the launch of our redesigned website. We serve patrons who live in our community and many who live outside our defined service boundaries. We found test subjects from both within and outside our service area and all of them easily found where the information on signing up for a library card was. What we realized was that our clear instructions on that page of our site had cut down on applications from nonlocal residents who were not supposed to be applying online (online registration was limited to patrons who lived in our service area, not for those registering cards from other towns). We kept the online application information as is with the intention of doing some advertising of the fact that residents could apply for library cards online, possibly in one of our home page "ad spaces."

USABILITY TESTING SCENARIO FOUR

You just heard the library has interactive electronic books for kids, called Tumblebooks. Find Tumblebooks.

We had the link to our Tumblebooks on the kids world page of our site, but found that the first place patrons looked for it was either with other downloadable books or in the database list. Since where we had the link to Tumblebooks was not where our patrons were looking for it, we added the link to those pages. We then tested again to be sure it could now be found.

USABILITY TESTING SCENARIO FIVE

You are interested in volunteering and becoming part of the Friends of the Library group. Find out information on the group and when their next meeting will take place.

Our Friends group was concerned that people couldn't easily find the information on their group now that they were not listed on the home page as they had been on our old site. Every patron we tested this scenario on could easily find the information on our Friends group, so we left things as they were and reassured our Friends group that people knew where to look for them.

As you can see, some of our usability testing led us to make changes to the site, and other times running the test reassured staff or groups associated with the library that the site was functioning as it was supposed to do. The scenarios listed above were all run with adults, but usability testing should also be undertaken with children, with teens, and with patrons who may have a disability and use assistive technology. If large portions of your service population speak another language, it is also a good idea to conduct the tests with them using the site in their native language.

> Conducting regular usability testing costs very little in terms of time and money, but can make a big difference in how well your website functions.

Conducting regular usability testing costs very little in terms of time and money, but can make a big difference in how well your website functions. It is also a necessary part of the iterative design process to keep your site the best it can be and put off another major website redesign project.

WEBSITE ANALYTICS

Another way to analyze how well your website is functioning is to take a look at the web analytics for your site. There are a number of tools out there to do this, but the most commonly used is the free service from Google called Google Analytics.

When looking at web analytics, you can find insights into things such as how many visitors your site gets daily, where those visitors are coming from, and how long they stay on your site. You can find out if they directly typed in your web address or used a search engine to find you, or even came to your website from one of your social media sites or a direct link you posted elsewhere. You can see on what pages people enter your website, how long they stay there, if they go to other pages within your site, or if they leave altogether after viewing the page they came in on. You can find out what pages on your websites get the most visits.

> When looking at web analytics, you can find out insights into things such as how many visitors your site gets daily, where those visitors are coming from, and how long they stay on your site.

You can also do some analysis of your visitors themselves. You can find out what browser they are using, and if they are using a computer or a mobile device to browse your site. You can look at whether they are new or returning visitors, and if they are return visitors, how long it has been since they last visited. You can see how many pages they view on an average visit and how long they stay there on your site.

The standard view when you first log into Google Analytics is for all visits in the past 30 days. You can easily change the time period you are viewing or look at a specific subset of all your visitors. Data can also be graphed in a variety of ways.

We use both Google Analytics and another analytics product called Crazy Egg. Crazy Egg has many of the same features of Google Analytics but also generates "heat maps" showing what people are doing on a specific page, such as which of your menu tabs gets clicked on the most. If you see tabs or links that are getting very little use, you can evaluate these items in your next round of usability testing or consider doing some promotion of that content.

Why should libraries care about the analytics for their website? Brian Clifton, in his book *Advanced Web Metrics with Google Analytics*, states, "With a better understanding of your website visitors you will be able to tailor page contents" (Clifton 2012, xxii). These analytics provide insight into why users are coming to your site and what they are doing once they get there. They can also provide information on which pages hold visitor attention for the longest period of time (which could mean you have a lot of interesting content there or it could mean people are very confused by what you are presenting them on that page). By looking at the browsers that your visitors use, you will know if there are older versions of browsers in which you should be testing your website to be sure that it works well in them. All of these insights can assist you in creating a website that works best for your users.

For information on Google Analytics, visit http://www.google.com/analytics/. For additional information on using the product, you can check out its Analytics Help Center at https://support.google.com/analytics/#topic=3544906. For more information on Crazy Egg, visit http://www.crazyegg.com/ where you can sign up for a free trial.

WEBSITE ANALYSIS AS PART OF YOUR OVERALL COMMUNICATIONS STRATEGY

Your website is your online digital branch, it is a marketing vehicle, and it is a communications tool. If your library conducts an annual communications review, your website should be included. Eisenhower Public Library District conducts an annual communications survey of patrons, which has shown that the website is one of the most popular ways for our patrons to get information about the library. This is important information to have to justify any budgeted monies that go toward personnel, or budget requests for the ongoing design and upkeep of your site. Results from your communications survey can also provide data you can use to create scenarios for your usability testing.

> If your library conducts an annual communications review, your website should be included.

- DO plan for ongoing usability testing after launch.
- DO use website analytics to gain insight into how your patrons are using your website.
- DO incorporate website analysis into your library's overall communications strategy.

RESOURCES

Clifton, Brian. *Advanced Web Metrics with Google Analytics*, 3rd ed. Indianapolis: John Wiley & Sons, 2012.
Krug, Steve. *Rocket Surgery Made Easy: The Do-It-Yourself Guide to Finding and Fixing Usability Problems*. Berkeley, CA: New Riders, 2010.

15

What We've Learned

Our aim in writing this book was to fill a gap in the literature that essentially would provide something of a road map for librarians who have taken on the responsibility—intentionally or otherwise—of becoming their library's webmaster or, at least, accidental web redesign project lead. Also, we wanted to provide our colleagues with the wisdom of our experience. In many ways, we felt very much as though we were feeling our way through this process. There were elements of it that were simply beyond our control. At the time, we were not responsible for the budget and therefore could only advise administration on how much we felt should be allocated to the project. We also went into it with the understanding that our choice of developer was already decided. We were somewhat unprepared for the extreme "drupalness" of Drupal (there really is not any other way to say it, and yes, it requires the invention of a new word), and for many things we needed to learn on the fly. We want to take this opportunity—as much for ourselves as for all of you—to summarize our experience and to reiterate what we learned, based on our successes and our missteps.

INTERVIEW MULTIPLE DEVELOPERS

Even if you think you know who you want to work with, take the time to meet with a number of web developers. This is never a bad idea. True professionals will understand the wisdom of this and appreciate that you are exploring all of your options. You may be able to reassure yourself and your administration that you are making the right choice or you may find someone who surprises you and changes your mind. And if you get multiple estimates of the cost of the project, you may be able to take those back to your first choice to see if they would be able to match the cost projection.

CHECK YOUR DEVELOPER'S REFERENCES

Take the time to check on the references that your web developer provides before signing a contract. Look at the websites that the developer has produced and talk with people who have previously used his or her services. Make sure others have been happy with the working relationship they had and the finished product that was delivered.

CLEARLY OUTLINE EXPECTATIONS WITH YOUR WEB DEVELOPER

There are several expectations that need to be outlined. Who will populate the pages with the content? Will the developer be available during the week leading up to your launch date, and will he or she be available all day, the day of your actual launch? Who will train the staff members responsible for the site's upkeep after the developer's responsibility has ended? Who will be the liaison? How will you be able to contact the developer with issues post-launch, and who is authorized to contact him or her? Is there a warrantee? What are the terms? All of these questions may seem like nit-picking, but they are vitally important before, during, and after the project. Trust us. We learned from experience on this one.

DO NOT SKIP THE ENVIRONMENTAL SCAN

Though you may feel that you know what is lacking in your current site and what you want to see in a new site, take the time to look at numerous library websites to see what others have done. Don't forget to take a look at nonlibrary websites too to see what features you can incorporate in your site. Take notes and make lists to share with your website developer. Look for both content and design features.

REMEMBER THAT FORM SHOULD FOLLOW FUNCTION

Concentrate first on the content that you want to include in your new website before you begin discussing the design. Evaluate the content of your current website and decide upon new content items to include. Look at the lists that you created during your survey of other websites. Start creating content as early as possible.

BEGIN FOSTERING STAFF BUY-IN ASAP

It is crucial to involve staff members and train them earlier in the process than you think, even before the formation of your project team. One of our biggest mistakes was to not start talking to the staff members who would be responsible for the creation and upkeep of elements of the site until just a few months before launch. Why was it a mistake? Because people are much more likely to take this seriously if they feel they have been consulted and included in some of the decision making. It is much harder to produce a quality product if you simply hand someone instructions and say, "make this." People who take pride in their work as a general rule appreciate having some input in the final product, even if it is minimal. You should identify and engage in a dialogue with these staff members immediately after you form your project team.

START THE CMS TRAINING CYCLE ONCE YOU DECIDE ON ONE

Once a content management system has been decided upon, training of key staff should begin immediately. That way, once content decisions have been made, staff will be able to begin populating pages. Training materials and your style guide should be readily and easily available to all staff working on the website. Procedures should also be put in place to train new staff members as they are hired.

GO WITH YOUR GUT

If your developer suggests something or is unwilling to change something that you know is wrong, do not back down. You are their boss, not the other way around. They are working for your library and you should have final say on your website. You know your patrons best, you deal with them everyday, and if you know in your gut that something is just not going to work for them, speak up. Do immediate usability testing on the item if you need data to back up your feelings.

EDIT MERCILESSLY

Thank you, Steve Krug. Nothing needs to be too wordy (except this book, but it wouldn't be if we made it into a website). Take a look at the content you have created and get rid of everything you can. Cut and cut again until only your essential message remains.

LET IT GO

As much as you may want some features, sometimes you just have to let them go if they aren't working well. While we really wanted to have beautiful bookshelves on many pages and a fantastic interactive book recommendation tool, they slowed the loading of our pages so much that we had to remove them. Mourn their loss, make a note of them for a future version of your website when your content management system can handle them, and move on.

TEST EARLY AND OFTEN

Thank you again, Steve Krug. This is some of the best advice we received/read when we embarked on this journey, and we still did not start this early enough. If we had, we may have identified the problem of the missing account log-in link before it became an issue to fix it. Even if your developer does not want you to show people the wireframes, do your absolute best to convince him or her otherwise. It is just as crucial to get your end users on board as it is to garner staff buy-in. This process is absolutely essential as a maintenance piece as well. Test the thing, and then test the change. Testing should continue as long as you have a library and as long as there is a library website.

LEARN HOW YOUR DESIGN WORKS

Be prepared to demonstrate the features of the new site and help users relearn how to do certain tasks. No matter how intuitive you think you have made something, someone will not understand. Also, in the teaching of the thing, you may discover ways in which you can improve it. That is not a bad thing. Make sure the front-line staff knows what is contained in the website and how it works. There is nothing more frustrating than hearing, "you should really put [insert anything you have already included in your website content here] on the site." We still get staff asking why we do not have some piece of information on the website and nine times out of ten, it is there. They just were not aware of it. This will probably happen no matter what you do or how thoroughly you train staff. People will quit and start, and it will affect how well your staff know your website. Still, it is worth it to make the effort to orient staff.

RESIGN YOURSELF TO A DELAYED LAUNCH DATE

Get yourself comfortable with the idea that it is more likely than not that your website will not launch on time. Prepare other stakeholders for this eventually by giving them a date range rather than an exact date. Don't announce a launch date to the public; just let them know it's coming. If you do manage to launch the site on time, pop open that bubbly and drink a toast to all involved.

RESPOND TO ALL USER COMMENTS

You need honest feedback and you should put a mechanism in place for users to easily comment on your site. Every comment should be responded to—

thank people for their positive comments, address comments about issues and correct them, and help those who are unsure about your site to become confident that everything will be okay. Be prepared for the fact that the comments are coming and have a plan in place to respond to them quickly.

PREPARE YOURSELF FOR NEGATIVITY

Be prepared for negative reactions from patrons and staff. It will hurt, and you will need to honestly evaluate every comment. If a real issue is brought to light, it will need to be dealt with. Other comments have no real solution; you are not going to go back to the old version of the site no matter what. Don't give yourself permission to turn those comments into a condemnation of your work. Sometimes people just don't like change and they will need time to adapt. Hopefully the positive comments you receive will more than balance out the negative ones.

MAKING ITERATIVE CHANGES IS KEY

Continue to make small changes and updates to keep the site fresh and lessen or forestall the need for an entire site redesign in the future. Test every change you make to ensure that it improves the site. Listen to suggestions from patrons and staff for ways in which to improve the site.

WATCH THAT TODDLER CLOSELY

Library websites are like toddlers (we wanted that to be the title of this book) —they need constant supervision. Drupal's "drupalness" caused us problems every time we turned our back on it—changing one thing had unexpected consequences, things seemed to move for no reason, and so on. We never knew what new issue we would encounter. Just like with a toddler, you need to keep a constant eye on it. While your experience with Drupal may be very different, we found this constant need for supervision as exhausting as having a toddler who keeps getting into trouble.

BE READY FOR THE TERRIBLE TWOS

At about the two-year mark, you will one day take a look at your website and think, "Here's what I would do differently if I were to design this website to-day." The two-year mark is a good time to do a full website inventory, evaluating each content item to see if it is being used or if it is content that you may want to consider changing or removing. While you should have been making iterative changes to keep the site fresh and up-to-date all along, the two-year mark is a good time to see if things are still working the way you originally intended. It was as we approached this two-year mark that we decided to switch content management systems due to our continued tussles with Drupal and to the fact that WordPress had become a more robust choice. We are not saying it is time for a redesign; it is just a good time for a full review.

TAKE WHAT YOU FIND HELPFUL

Not every lesson will be applicable to every library website, so use what you will from what we have learned. We hope that you find something that makes a difference in your experience with this process. Feel free to contact us to let us know if we helped you or if you have any questions for us. Tell us we were wrong, or tell us we were right. We're still learning too! We look forward to hearing from you and will be sure to respond.

Afterword

Until we began this book, we never realized how lengthy the process of writing a book could be. From our presentation at Internet Librarian in October 2013 to the publication of what you hold in your hands, the process has taken just over two years. Two years may not seem that long, but in terms of technology, a lot can change in that time. From 2013 to now, Joomla has gone from being a strong contender for an open source content management system choice to a distant third behind Drupal and WordPress among library websites in our library system. Websites featuring Pinterest-style cards have become so extremely popular in website design that they are already on their way out, and in the two years since the launch of our new website, we have made quite a few changes to it as well.

If you have browsed over our website while reading this book, you may have noticed that it looks somewhat different than the screenshots we have included. Over time we had removed some items from the site that weren't working well (bookshelves, book recommendation tool, etc.) and made other minor changes that came about as suggestions during our usability testing. The biggest change we are in the process of making to the current site is in our content management system.

The idiosyncratic nature of Drupal—i.e., its "drupalness"—made it hard for us to work with our website in-house, as no one on staff was a true Drupal expert. This drupalness meant that while our web designer and web-masters knew quite a bit about Drupal, there would be inexplicable things that would just seem to happen to cause havoc to our website. Lesson learned: knowing "quite a bit" about Drupal does not in any sense make anyone a true Drupal expert. Our website committee made the decision to move from Drupal to WordPress to make the site easier to work with. WordPress has made great strides in the two-plus years since we first made our decision to redesign our website in 2012. We have seen other libraries use the content management system to produce astoundingly beautiful websites with none of the fussiness that we have consistently encountered. That greatly influenced our decision. This time our graphics and web designer is redesigning the site in-house, teaching himself WordPress along the way. We were not in a position to hire an outside website developer, nor did we want to, and having someone on staff who could and was willing to learn WordPress meant we did not have to.

We are trying to mirror the look of the 2013 website in this iteration, since we still like the overall design. We did try to make improvements to the usability, of course. We've kept the navigation menus at the top, kept the photo rotator and the "ad space" content boxes, and made the look a little cleaner while still keeping the same "feel." We had found out from surveys that patrons and staff wanted our hours and location information at the top of the page, so we put them there. We had a moment of "we told you so" because this was something we had wanted to do when we first redesigned the site in 2013 and our developer talked us out of it. We increased the size of the search box to make it easier to use, which was another element we were talked out of during the original design phase. We changed some of the choices in our menus based on feedback from users to make the choices as logical and easy to use as possible. We will be moving items down to our footer instead of burying them in menus that did not seem to make sense to users during usability testing. We are eliminating the departmental blogs and decided to go with one library-wide blog that just about anyone could contribute to. We did usability testing on the changes right away, first with staff and then with patrons. The information gained from our ongoing usability testing had made the site the best it could be, and this change of content management systems feels like one more step in the iterative design process rather than a total redesign.

We have received favorable comments from those who have used the newest version of our website during usability testing, along with constructive comments and comments that made us realize that, even among our staff, sometimes things just do not translate. We invite you to take a look at the current version of our website and compare it to the screenshots of the 2013 version of the site. It will never be perfect, and that is part of the thrill of a project like redesigning a website. The definitions of "good" and "better" in the context of website design and development continue to evolve. Perfection means something that does not ever need to change. When things stop changing, they eventually stop being relevant, and then we end up back where we were at the beginning of this book, with a website that is dated and a lot of work ahead of us. The process of writing this book helped us get through this admittedly large iterative change to our own website—there is nothing like learning from your mistakes—and we hope reading this book helps our readers navigate the ever-changing process of producing a website that patrons love to use, and librarians are proud to show off.

Appendix

MARKETING PLAN FOR EISENHOWER PUBLIC LIBRARY WEBSITE

EISENHOWERLIBRARY.ORG
"EISENHOWER 24/7"

Situation Analysis

In May 2013, Eisenhower Public Library District launched a newly redesigned website. The new website is intended to be the library's "virtual branch" and will be marketed under the slogan "Eisenhower 24/7." A marketing plan is needed to inform users about the new site, promote the new features of the site, and increase traffic to the site. The site went live on May 2, 2013, with a "soft launch," and a full marketing campaign will take place starting in June.

Target Audience

- Eisenhower Public Library District staff
- Current patrons of the library
- Residents of Norridge and Harwood Heights
- Teens

Key Messages

- This redesign is in response to patron input (in person and by survey response).
- The website is a "virtual branch" of the library.
- This virtual branch is available 24 hours a day, 7 days a week from anywhere.
- Responsive design makes the site available on all computers and devices.
- Reorganization and new features make the site more informative and easier to use.

- Usability testing will lead to continued improvements to the site.
- A new calendar interface is phase II of the project.

New Features of the Site to Promote

- Home page: photo rotator, Library News section, Upcoming Events list, New Arrivals bookshelf, ad spaces
- "I Want . . . a Great Read" book recommendation tool
- "Sticky" menu on interior pages
- Our collection section with areas for adults, teens, and kids
- Research section
- Programs & Events is the new calendar
- Connect with Us page and Get Involved section
- How Do I? section
- Community section
- Local History digital collection and blog
- Personalized Book Recommendation form

Goals

- ❖ **Increase awareness of the website redesign and new site features**
  - ➢ Objective: All patrons in Norridge and Harwood Heights should be aware of the site redesign and its features
    - ▪ Strategy and tactics: Multiformat marketing blitz including print materials, social media and website information blurbs, and demonstrations
- ❖ **Increase traffic to the site**
  - ➢ Objective: Have more patrons use the site and become repeat visitors
    - ▪ Strategy and tactics: Keep site dynamic by updating content on a weekly basis; increase visibility and ranking using search engine optimization to drive traffic from online search engines
- ❖ **Increase patron interaction with all electronic media (website blogs and social media)**
  - ➢ Objective: To create a two-way dialogue between the library and its patrons
    - ▪ Strategy and tactics: Use the website to drive visitors to our social media outlets and those outlets to drive traffic to the website; weekly book reviews with the ability for patrons to comment; teens able to submit their own book reviews on teen blog
- ❖ **Promote sign-ups for new e-mail newsletter**
  - ➢ Objective: To increase the number of patrons signed up to receive our monthly e-mail newsletter
    - ▪ Strategy and tactics: Promote the e-mail newsletter in print and online

❖ **Make ongoing incremental changes to keep the site fresh**
  ➤ Objective: To avoid a major redesign in the future
    ▪ Strategy and tactics: Ongoing monthly usability testing to make small changes on an ongoing basis

Promotion

- **Photo rotator slide**—Branding of "Eisenhower 24/7" and link to ask for feedback (*starting day of launch: May 2, 2013*)

- **Computer monitor signs**—Placed on each computer monitor with access to the internet (*starting day of launch: May 2, 2013*)

- **Newsletter**—Cover image and "Explore . . ." article focused on new website in the Spring 2013 issue of the Eisenhower Explorer newsletter (*mid-May*)

- **Lobby monitor**—Slides advertising new website—announcement of it and then highlighting features (*May and June*)

- **Bookmarks**—Bookmarks highlighting the new features of our website will be available at all service desks with versions specific to adults, young adults, and kids

- **Posters**—Placed throughout the library

- **Postcards**—Passed out in the library, at local events, and at meetings of other community groups: Rotary, Chamber of Commerce, etc.; check with Harlem Irving Plaza to see if we could pass our postcards to shoppers

- **Press releases**—Sent to all media contacts; personal follow-up call to local reporters

- **Demonstrations**—Will include a table set up in the lobby or library services area, staffed by two staff members with two laptop computers; demo times will be in two-hour shifts at various times (mornings, afternoons, evenings, weekends) to show patrons new features of the redesigned website and answer any questions they may have about using the site; demonstrations can be proposed for the Chamber of Commerce and Rotary meetings (*late May–early June*)

- **Farmers market demos and handouts**—Increase awareness of and traffic to the site (*June 19 and July 17*)

- **Website brochure**—Overview of the website and its features

- **Realtor/New resident brochure**—Overview of the website and the library

- **Ridgewood High School newsletter ad**—To try to get teen traffic to new website

- **Social media cross-marketing**—Increase traffic from our social media sites to the website

References and
Additional Resources

BOOKS

Clark, Joe. *Building Accessible Web Sites*. Berkeley, CA: New Riders, 2002.

Clifton, Brian. *Advanced Web Metrics with Google Analytics* (3rd ed.). Indianapolis, IN: John Wiley & Sons, 2012.

Horton, Sarah, and Whitney Qusenberg. *A Web for Everyone: Designing Accessible User Experiences*. Brooklyn, NY: Rosenfeld Media, 2014.

Kalbach, James. *Designing Web Navigation*. Sebastopol, CA: O'Reilly Media, 2007.

Krug, Steve. *Don't Make Me Think, Revisited: A Common Sense Approach to Web and Mobile Usability*. Berkeley, CA: New Riders, 2014.

Krug, Steve. *Rocket Surgery Made Easy: The Do-It-Yourself Guide to Finding and Fixing Usability Problems*. Berkeley, CA: New Riders, 2010.

Lynch, Patrick J., and Sarah Horton. *Web Style Guide: Basic Design Principles for Creating Web Sites* (3rd ed.). New Haven, CT: Yale University Press, 2008.

Morville, Peter, and Louis Rosenfeld. *Information Architecture for the World Wide Web*. Sebastopol, CA: O'Reilly Media, 2007.

Nielsen, Jakob, and Hoa Loranger. *Prioritizing Web Usability*. Berkeley, CA: New Riders, 2006.

Nielsen, Jakob, and Marie Tahir. *Homepage Usability: 50 Websites Deconstructed*. Berkeley, CA: New Riders, 2000.

Redish, Janice. *Letting Go of the Words: Writing Web Content That Works* (2nd ed.). Waltham, MA: Morgan Kaufmann, 2014.

Zeldman, Jeffrey, and Ethan Marcotte. *Designing with Web Standards* (3rd ed.). Berkeley, CA: New Riders, 2010.

WEBSITES

Advanced Common Sense: https://www.sensible.com/downloads-rsme.html

American Fact Finder: http://factfinder.census.gov/

American Library Association Value Calculator: http://www.ala.org/advocacy/advleg/advocacyuniversity/toolkit/makingthecase/library_calculator

Analytics Help Center: https://support.google.com/analytics/#topic=3544906

City-Data.com: http://www.city-data.com/

Crazy Egg: http://www.crazyegg.com/

Create a Website Style Guide: http://www.creativebloq.com/design/create-website-style-guide-6123030

Designing Style Guides for Brands and Websites: http://www.smashingmagazine.com/2010/07/21/designing-style-guidelines-for-brands-and-websites/

Develop a Style Guide for Your Site: http://www.sitepoint.com/develop-style-guide-site/

Google Analytics: http://www.google.com/analytics/

Google Translate: https://translate.google.com/manager/website/

How to Prepare a Style Guide for Your Website: http://www.wix.com/blog/2010/11/how-to-prepare-a-style-guide-for-your-website/

Internet Archive: Wayback Machine: https://archive.org/web/

"Library Refashions Its Website," *Chicago Tribune*. April 11, 2014: ProQuest: http://search.proquest.com/docview/1514686847/C77F60234A3D4551PQ/1?accountid=58103

"The Mission and Role of the Library Website," Stover, Mark. 1997: http://misc.library.ucsb.edu/universe/stover.html

Must Have Website Style Guide Content: http://www.collaborint.com/resources/website_planning/styleguide_content.asp

MyBestSegments: https://www.claritas.com/MyBestSegments/Default.jsp?ID=20

10 Essentials to Keep Web Readers Engaged: http://www.ragan.com/Main/Articles/10_essentials_to_keep_Web_readers_engaged_45425.aspx

The Web at 25 in the U.S.: http://www.pewinternet.org/2014/02/27/the-web-at-25-in-the-u-s/

20 Tips for Writing for the Web: http://www.fatdux.com/blog/2009/08/07/20-tips-for-writing-for-the-web/

Web Writing Style Guide: http://www.hampshire.edu/web-writing-style-guide.htm

Index

About the Authors

STACY ANN WITTMANN, MLIS, is the library director of Eisenhower Public Library District in Harwood Heights, Illinois. She worked with Julie to redesign Eisenhower Public Library District's website and co-presented on web design at the Internet Librarian Conference in 2013. Stacy earned her MLIS from the University of Illinois Urbana-Champaign. She is a member of the American Library Association, the Public Library Association, and the Illinois Library Association. Stacy has presented programs at the Internet Librarian Conference in 2014 and 2015.

JULIANNE T. STAM, MLIS, is the marketing specialist at Eisenhower Public Library District in Harwood Heights, Illinois. Julie holds an MBA in marketing research from DePaul University and earned her MLIS from Drexel University. She is a member of the American Library Association, the Public Library Association, and the Illinois Library Association. Julie has presented programs at recent ALA and ILA conferences. She worked with Stacy to coordinate the redesign of Eisenhower's website and co-presented on web design at the Internet Librarian Conference in 2013.